101+
Complaint Letters
That
Get Results

Second Edition

Janet Rubel
Attorney at Law

SPHINX® PUBLISHING
AN IMPRINT OF SOURCEBOOKS, INC.®
NAPERVILLE, ILLINOIS
www.SphinxLegal.com

Second Edition: 2006

Published by: **Sphinx® Publishing, An Imprint of Sourcebooks, Inc.®**

Naperville Office
P.O. Box 4410
Naperville, Illinois 60567-4410
630-961-3900
Fax: 630-961-2168
www.sourcebooks.com
www.SphinxLegal.com

This publication is designed to provide accurate and authoritative information in regard to the subject matter covered. It is sold with the understanding that the publisher is not engaged in rendering legal, accounting, or other professional service. If legal advice or other expert assistance is required, the services of a competent professional person should be sought.

From a Declaration of Principles Jointly Adopted by a Committee of the American Bar Association and a Committee of Publishers and Associations

This product is not a substitute for legal advice.

Disclaimer required by Texas statutes.

Library of Congress Cataloging-in-Publication Data

Rubel, Janet.
  101+ complaint letters that get results / by Janet Rubel. -- 2nd ed.
     p. cm.
  First ed. has title: 101 complaint letters that get results.
  ISBN-13: 978-1-57248-563-1 (pbk. : alk. paper)
  ISBN-10: 1-57248-563-9 (pbk. : alk. paper)
  1. Complaint letters. 2. Consumer complaints.   I. Title. II. Title:
  One hundred one plus complaint letters that get results. III. Title:
 One hundred and one plus complaint letters that get results.
  HF5415.52.R83 2006
  381.3--dc22
                                                    2006022329

Printed and bound in the United States of America.
SB — 10 9 8 7 6 5 4 3 2 1

I dedicate this book to my husband, Alan, and my daughters, Amanda, following in my footsteps in the law, and Rebecca, doing good deeds of *tikkun olam*, to improve our world, and to Matthew Portes, my soon-to-be son-in-law.

Acknowledgments

Thank you to my editor, Sarah Brittin, for her helpful suggestions and hard work. I am grateful, too, to everyone at Sphinx Publishing and Sourcebooks, Inc. for their efforts and support of this book.

I throw a "good" tile to my Mah Jong friends for their good humor and friendship at our weekly games.

Contents

Chapter 4: Employment 53

Chapter 5: Finances 73

Chapter 6: Identity Theft and Computer-Based Fraud 103

Identity Theft

Phishing

Pretexting

Stolen Purses, Briefcases, and Luggage

Patients Victimized

Taking Action—Step-by-Step

How to Access the Letters on the Website

Thank you for purchasing *101+ Complaint Letters That Get Results*. In this book, we have worked hard to compile exactly what you need to write an effective complaint letter. To make this material even more useful, we have included every sample letter in the book on our website, at **www.sphinxlegal.com/extras/ComplaintLetters**.

You can modify these letters for your personal use. Simply choose the letter that you feel most accurately represents your situation, and change all of the information to fit your own particular needs. You can even use them over and over again, or choose a different letter if another situation arises that warrants action.

The downloadable letters are compatible with both PC and Mac operating systems. (While they should work with either operating system, we cannot guarantee that they will work with your particular system, and we cannot provide technical assistance.) To use the letters on your computer, you will need to use Microsoft Word or another word processing program that can read Word files. The website does not contain any such program.

Go online to **www.sphinxlegal.com/extras/ComplaintLetters**, and click on "Downloads." All of the letters are downloadable by chapter. (For example, all of the letters for Chapter 2 can be found in a single Word document titled "Chapter

2: Cars.") Once you have located the letter packet to download, simply click on the appropriate link.

The information provided in the letters is only a reference guide to assist you in completing one for your situation, and any information that is not applicable should be removed from your final version. Once all of your information is filled in, you can print your letter.

Purchasers of this book are granted a license to use the forms contained in it for their own personal use. By purchasing this book, you have also purchased a limited license to use all forms from this book made available at **www.sphinxlegal.com/extras/ComplaintLetters**. The license limits you to personal use only and all other copyright laws must be adhered to. No claim of copyright is made in any government form reproduced in the book or available at **www.sphinxlegal.com/extras/ComplaintLetters**. You are free to modify the forms and tailor them to your specific situation.

The author and publisher have attempted to provide the most current and up-to-date information available. However, the courts, Congress, and your state's legislatures review, modify, and change laws on an ongoing basis, as well as create new laws from time to time. Due to the very nature of the information and the continual changes in our legal system, to be sure that you have the current and best information for your situation, you should consult a local attorney or research the current laws yourself.

This publication is designed to provide accurate and authoritative information. It is sold with the understanding that the publisher is not engaged in rendering legal, accounting, or other professional service. If legal advice or other expert assistance is required, the services of a competent professional person should be sought.

—*From a Declaration of Principles Jointly Adopted by a Committee of the American Bar Association and a Committee of Publishers and Associations*

This product is not a substitute for legal advice.

—*Disclaimer required by Texas statutes*

Introduction

There have been incredible changes in the law since the first edition of this book. Many additions have been made to this second edition to correspond with the rapid changes in our society and the laws. The Do Not Call Registry is now in effect all across the country. Computer crime has become a significant problem. Spoofing, phishing, scamming, stealing data from legitimate companies, buying phony telephone caller identification to deceive consumers, and other schemes have become pervasive. In response, information has been added—sometimes entirely new chapters—to help you understand your rights in regards to the new laws.

Along with new information to help you understand your rights, a new chapter has been added to outline the basics of writing an effective complaint letter. This chapter guides you through the entire process, and provides helpful tips to make your letter successful. There is also a new chapter that provides help if the complaint letters do not achieve the intended result. Information about complaining to the appropriate government agency and taking your case to small claims court is included.

On top of all these brand-new additions, this book has expanded greatly on the previous edition. New letters have been added to all chapters. The appendices have been updated and expanded to provide the most up-to-date information possible.

A new appendix has been added to include information about federal agencies useful to the consumer.

Each chapter is divided into two sections—the consumer reference summary and the sample letters. Each letter is completed for a specific incident to demonstrate the appropriate wording for a particular type of complaint.

This book is unique in that it contains information you can use to understand your rights as a consumer, and samples of letters that are both in the book and available on our website, so that you can edit and print your own letter from your computer.

Caveat emptor—let the buyer beware—is as true today as it was in ancient times. The type of theft is more sophisticated and often done with a few keystrokes, but the principle is the same: watch your money!

Misfortune can strike at any point in your life. Whether it is a recurring problem with a car or a billing problem with a credit card company, there are numerous things that can go wrong. Sometimes it is difficult to resolve even the simplest matters because anger or frustration gets in the way. The letters and information in this book will help you find a solution by taking the emotion out of the complaint.

• • • • •

AUTHOR'S NOTE: *This book is intended to be a guide for consumers, but is not intended to be legal advice. You should consult your own legal advisor to obtain information pertinent to your situation. If you cannot afford an attorney, you may qualify for legal aid. Call your local bar association for details. For those who cannot qualify for legal aid, there may be help available at law school clinics or charitable legal assistance clinics. Ask your local reference librarian for resource information, or look on the Internet for lawyers who handle certain problems without requiring payment.*

1

How to Write a Complaint Letter

Writing an effective complaint letter is a skill that everyone needs to perfect in this fast-paced, impersonal society. Today, most people do not deal with the owners of the businesses that we patronize. Many stores are owned by large corporations headquartered hundreds or thousands of miles away. As big box stores and mergers and acquisitions gobble up local department stores and grocery stores, it becomes much less likely that people know the owners of the stores in their neighborhoods.

The need for an effective complaint letter is not limited to shopping problems. Certain complaints must be sent the old fashioned way—in writing—in order to protect your legal rights. These problems include credit card disputes, banking mistakes, insurance disputes, landlord/tenant issues, and others. The careful consumer reads the fine print on all documents and sends the appropriate type of complaint letter in the required manner.

The beauty of sending a complaint letter is that you can have legal proof that you have sent the letter. It is difficult for a company to deny receiving your complaint letter when you can produce a certified mail receipt from the United States Postal Service. If a certified letter is not required to present your complaint, it is still often a sound idea to spend the three or four dollars to send the letter.

Writing an effective complaint letter is not complicated. Follow the steps discussed in this chapter and you will be on your way to consumer assertiveness.

STEP ONE—GATHER ANY RELEVANT DOCUMENTS

Relevant documents include receipts, sales contracts, warranties, extended warranties, insurance policies, and bills. Never throw these important documents away. Make photocopies of these documents to send with your complaint letter. You should *never* send the originals unless it is required. *Always* keep copies of any originals you have to send. If you have to send an original, send it via certified mail or registered mail.

STEP TWO—THINK

Writing an effective complaint letter requires you to focus on the problem and the result you want to obtain. If you have an appliance that is under warranty, do you want it repaired or replaced? Have the expensive shoes you purchased at a department store with a limited return policy failed to withstand normal wear and tear after the required return date? Is your employer denying you family leave that you are entitled to under the law? Do you want your landlord to fix a problem in your apartment, or permit you to have it repaired and receive a credit on your next month's rent?

STEP THREE—WRITE A ROUGH DRAFT

Do not send the first letter that comes to mind. Write a first draft. Read it over to make sure that you have described the problem and are clear about the result you want. Make sure your letter minimally includes your telephone number and address.

Try to engage the recipient of your letter in your problem. Use the model of, "I have a problem. Could you please help me?" Your first complaint letter on any topic should be reasonable and to the point. Be sure to thank the recipient for his or her help, even if you doubt that you will receive it.

Keep the letter brief—no more than one page. Break your letter into separate paragraphs. Double-space your letter if it is written on the computer. If you have to handwrite your letter, make sure your writing is legible.

Absolutely no foul language is allowed. Try not to use slang. Do not use a lot of exclamation points. Do not use *emoticons* (smiley faces) if you are drafting this on your computer. Check the spelling of your letter—do not rely only on the automatic spell checking software on your computer. Use a dictionary if you need to look up a word. Be sure to use correct grammar.

If you never learned how to write a correct business letter (or have forgotten), then you need to use the letters in this book as a model, or get a good reference book from the library or bookstore. A business letter should contain a heading for you (name, address, and telephone number), the date of the letter, the address of the person or company to whom your complaint is directed, a notation to indicate what the letter is regarding, and the correct salutation. Salutations such as "Dear Sir," "Dear Madame," "Dear Ms.," or "To whom it may concern" are acceptable today.

You should try to determine who the correct person to send the complaint letter to is if it is not provided for you. This can be very difficult sometimes. Other times, it is as easy as picking up the telephone and calling the company. If the company is state regulated, check with the appropriate state licensing authority, such as the Department of Financial Institutions, secretary of state, or Department of Insurance.

STEP FOUR—WRITE THE FINAL DRAFT

Read through your letter again. It is acceptable to express your unhappiness or disappointment with the product or service, but do not be emotional or hysterical. Be businesslike in your approach. Check your spelling, grammar, and tone.

Again, the letter should not exceed one page if possible. The reader will not pay attention to a lengthy letter. Remember that most large companies receive hundreds of pieces of correspondence each day. You do not want your letter to be tossed into the circular file.

STEP FIVE—SEND THE LETTER

Do not send your letter through email as your sole method of communication. You may email your complaint letter to the appropriate person or department, as long as you send a hard copy via U.S. mail or an express delivery service. Be sure to use the correct mode of delivery for your complaint (if certified mail is required, then do not send it any other way). Enclose the relevant documents, and never send the originals unless you are required to do so. For more information on how to correctly note any inclusions, see page 8.

STEP SIX—FOLLOW UP

Mark your calendar to remind yourself to look for a response to your letter in two weeks. It is reasonable to allow ten business days or so to pass before taking the next step.

Note: *You should not wait two weeks for a response if this is an urgent matter, such as obtaining approval for medication from your health insurance company or a referral from your HMO for medical care.*

If you have not received the satisfaction desired or any response to your letter after two weeks, then you should consider what to do next. Double-check to make sure that you did not forget to mail the letter or send the fax, or that your letter came back for postage due. Determine if there is another department or person to whom you should address your complaint. You should always try to have the name of a person to contact for assistance.

Many big companies have public relations personnel or special response teams accountable to the president or chief executive officer of the corporation. You may have to call the company to obtain this information. Another possibility is to contact the media relations department. There is usually someone in this department who can expedite a resolution to your problem by cutting through company red tape.

If you cannot get a response or satisfaction, consider sending your complaint via certified mail. Sometimes this gets attention, because the mail room is instructed to treat this mail differently from other mail. It may be forwarded to the legal department or an executive instead of sitting on someone's desk.

You may wish to make a telephone call to the company. This is harder than ever today because of voice mail. The customer is placed on hold for interminable periods of time, and then is sometimes disconnected. You are often lucky to connect with a real human.

Companies treat customers this way as a concerted strategy to discourage complaints. They figure that if the process is difficult, many people will give up. It is also cheaper for the company to do without customer service employees.

STEP SEVEN—COMPLAIN TO THE APPROPRIATE GOVERNMENT AGENCY

Many professions and businesses are licensed by the state and federal governments. Attorneys, doctors, hospitals, plumbers, contractors, moving companies, banks, and collection agencies are among those that require licenses. Hospitals and nursing homes are regulated by the states in which they are located, and they may also be accredited by national groups. Insurance companies are also regulated by the states in which they operate. Check with your state for a list of professions with licensing requirements.

Federal agencies require businesses affecting interstate commerce, such as moving companies, to have a license. Also, federal agencies, such as the Federal Trade Commission (FTC), regulate debt collection practices and mail order practices (when items must be shipped, what the seller must do if the item is not in stock, and so on). Banks can be regulated by the state or federal government. A bank with *State Bank* in its title is regulated by the state. A bank with *Federal* or *National* in its title is regulated by the United States (federal) government.

Filing a complaint will not necessarily resolve your complaint. However, the agency may take action on your behalf and remedy your problem. If nothing else, the company or individual may lose its license to operate. The complaint will be part of the public record, so others can learn of the problems you experienced.

Another possibility is to file a complaint with your local *Better Business Bureau* (BBB). The Better Business Bureau is a nonprofit group that works to prevent dishonest business practices and conducts a complaint resolution service for various problems, including many discussed in this book. Look in your local telephone book or search the Internet for your local chapter. The BBB has no legal authority to hear your complaint, order a company to return your money, or perform the necessary services for you. However, it will note your problem, even if not necessarily resolving your complaint—which sometimes will make a business act.

The final chapter of this book covers the process of complaining to a government agency and pursuing legal action in greater detail. Check Appendix E for a list of state and federal agencies that oversee common businesses and professions.

STEP EIGHT—TAKE LEGAL ACTION

You may decide that legal action is necessary. This should be your last resort. If you choose to go to court, there are a number of alternatives, which are discussed in more detail in Chapter 12.

Small Claims Court

Every state court system has a small claims court. It may be known by other names locally, but there is a court devoted to cases under a certain dollar amount, where consumers may act as their own attorneys. These courts are designed to allow consumers to resolve complaints on their own. There are user-friendly forms provided, and the judges try to run a more relaxed courtroom in order to enable litigants without lawyers to pursue their cases. When a person acts as his or her own attorney, he or she is said to be acting *pro se*. (This is pronounced "pro say," for the Latin "acting for oneself.")

Deciding where to file your case can be a problem. Does the company have a local store or office? Did you buy on the Internet? Does the fine print of any contract or sales agreement require you to file suit in a certain state? Are you required to submit your complaint to binding arbitration? The answers to these questions can determine where your case should be filed.

Hire a Lawyer

You should consider hiring an attorney to represent you if you cannot navigate the court system on your own. Many small claims courts allow attorneys to represent parties. If there is an attorney on the other side, you should consider hiring one to represent you. If you act without an attorney, you are presumed to know the law.

If your case involves enough money, you might be able to interest a lawyer in representing you on a *contingency* basis. This means that the lawyer will not collect a fee unless you win. However, you will probably be required to pay court costs, such as filing fees. The amount of a contingency fee varies, but is generally 25% to 33% of the amount collected, or one-fourth to one-third. Call your local bar association for a referral or ask a friend for a recommendation.

Even if you can win your case against the other side, you might not know how to collect on the final order or judgment. There are very strict laws governing the collection of a debt. You can land yourself in big trouble trying to collect your debt if you do not follow those rules. Having an attorney in such a situation can be very helpful.

EFFECTIVE LETTERS

Writing an effective complaint letter is an art. Anyone can write an expletive-laced, angry letter. The key is to write a brief, simple, and convincing letter stating the facts, the problem, and the result you want to achieve. It is also imperative to include copies of the necessary and relevant documents, such as receipts. Remember to black out any credit card numbers and your Social Security number except for the last four digits, unless absolutely necessary to resolve your problem.

To make your letter more formal, you may wish to indicate that certain things are being included with your letter, or that something more is being done with it. You can indicate this at the bottom of your letter, under your name and signature, by adding certain designations to your letter.

Whenever you include copies of important documents—something you should always do to make your complaint more effective—it is often helpful to indicate on the letter that you have done so. You can do this by adding the word "enclosure" or the abbreviation "enc." This also tells the reader of the letter that something more was sent with it, and that they should make sure they review that material as well.

Sometimes it takes more than your first letter to get the results you want. Sometimes more action happens when the letter is sent to more than one person, such as multiple people in the organization or a governmental entity. It is proper to indicate everyone the letter is sent to, usually by using the antiquated designation of "carbon copy" or "cc," and indicating after the "cc" who the other party or parties were that the letter was sent to.

Finally, you should always keep a hard copy of the letter. You can indicate that you have done so by adding "file" at the end of your letter, showing that you are keeping a file of this matter. You do not have to show this, but it tells the reader that you are serious and keeping good records. It is always a good idea to keep a hard copy of your communication, in case something happens to your computer.

If you were to write a letter with a receipt enclosed, copied to the recipient's manager, and printed a copy for your file, the bottom of your letter might appear as follows:
Your Name
enc: Receipt
cc: Manager's Name
file

NOTE: *Addressing a letter to the legal department or to the General Counsel's office at a large company routes the letter directly to the lawyers.*

Sample Letters

The three letters in this chapter illustrate the types of letters to send when a problem is not resolved. The first letter is very simple and light in tone, the second letter is direct and more businesslike, and the third letter is very firm with legal action threatened. You will note that the second and the third letters are sent via certified mail to leave a paper trail of proof of the consumer's attempts to resolve the problem. The certified mail receipts will be helpful to the consumer if legal action is necessary. Judges are not sympathetic to companies when court action is required to make them do the right thing. You may be able to recover attorney's fees and costs if you have to hire a lawyer.

Fact Pattern

Each of the letters follows the same fact pattern. The homeowner, David Berke, sold his home. He notified his utility companies of the sale, and moved into his new home. However, the gas company failed to transfer his bill to the name of the buyer. David continued to be billed months after he moved, and the gas company eventually turned his account over to collection and placed negative information in his credit file.

In this situation, David (the homeowner) should also obtain a copy of his credit report to ensure that the utility company removed the incorrect information. If this information is not removed from the file by the utility company, then he should write to the credit reporting agencies disputing the information and requesting that it be deleted. If this is not done by the credit reporting agency within roughly thirty days, then the homeowner may have a nice lawsuit against the utility company and the credit reporting agency. (For more on credit reporting, see Chapter 5.)

Letter 1.1:
Humorous

David Berke
11386 Clavey Road
Glencoe, IL 60035
606-414-7272

August 8, 2007

Unfriendly Gas Company
P.O. Box 60825
Chicago, IL 60601

Re: Error in Billing

Dear Sir or Madam:

On January 4, 2007, I moved to my new home in Glencoe, IL. I notified the post office and all utilities, including yours, of the move. All utility companies except your company have delivered final bills for service for my former address. I have called your customer service office repeatedly, but elves must be working in that office. All evidence of my calls has vanished. Each person I speak with there claims to have no record of my calls or move.

Believe me, I have not been cloned! You are billing me for residential gas use at my old address and my new one. Please correct this error. Enclosed is a copy of proof of notification to you of the house sale.

Thank you,

The Real David Berke

Letter 1.2:
Direct

David Berke
11386 Clavey Road
Glencoe, IL 60035
606-414-7272

August 18, 2007

Unfriendly Gas Company
P.O. Box 60825
Chicago, IL 60601

Re: Error in Billing

Dear Sir or Madam:

I wrote to you on August 8, 2007, to complain that there is an error in billing. A copy of that letter is enclosed. I had high hopes that you would resolve the problem, but that has not occurred. Today I received another bill along with a note that you are turning the account over for collection. I dispute the accuracy of the bill and demand that you correct the account, including contacting the collection agency to advise of the error. You must correct any negative information you have placed in my credit file and/or reported to third parties.

Once again, I am advising you that the buyer of my former residence should be billed for service after the sale of the home, not I. This problem has not been solved after eight months. If you do not correct this problem within five business days, I shall have no choice but to take legal action against you. I trust that this will not be necessary.

Very truly yours,

David Berke
Via certified mail #8307409121

Letter 1.3:
Legal Action

David Berke
11386 Clavey Road
Glencoe, IL 60035
606-414-7272

August 28, 2007

Unfriendly Gas Company
General Counsel
P.O. Box 60825
Chicago, IL 60601

Re: Error in Billing

Dear Counselor:

Enclosed please find a copy of each of my previous two letters to the customer service department at your company, along with a list of the dates, times, and persons with whom I spoke there about the error in my billing.

Your company has failed to resolve this matter. In addition, now you have placed negative information in my credit file and turned the account over to a collection agency. You have violated the federal Fair Debt Collection Practices Act by continuing to pursue this matter. You have besmirched my good name and my credit standing.

Therefore, I plan to take legal action against you to collect damages and attorney's fees, as well as costs incurred to rectify this travesty. I am filing complaints with the attorney general's office, utilities regulators, Better Business Bureau, and other private and public agencies.

Very truly yours,

David Berke
Via certified mail #4390064182

2
Cars

For most people, a car is one of the most expensive items they will ever purchase or lease. A car is necessary for many people to commute to work, take children to school and their many activities, and for convenience.

Car dealers are a source of many consumer complaints—from bogus processing fees added to the sales contract, to defective repairs and unreliable new cars. Consult the federal, state, and local laws to determine the permitted fees and charges. Dealers may try to increase their profit by adding fees, such as loan processing, warehousing, advertising, paperwork, administrative costs, or other pure profit items. You do not have to pay any of these fees. Read your financial documents very carefully.

LEMON LAWS

State and federal laws exist to protect consumers from defective new cars, shoddy repairs, and used car sales. The state and federal laws that protect the consumer from defective new cars are called *lemon laws.*

There are state and federal laws that require automobile dealers and manufacturers to repair or replace defective new cars. If you have the misfortune of buying such a car, learn your rights under your state laws. The state where you purchased the car is the applicable law to follow. Your state's attorney general can provide helpful information about the law and your rights as a car purchaser and owner. Large cities often have their own consumer departments and laws concerning cars. An excellent website with links to each state's law is **www.nationallemonlawcenter.com**.

Each state has its own laws and rules that must be followed in order to preserve your rights. For example, some states require the dealer to make three attempts to fix the car before you can demand a new car. Other states require four visits before the dealer must replace the lemon.

Many states require the dealer to give you a new car or to refund your purchase price if you have purchased a lemon. When taking in your car for repairs, always get a written work order that specifies that you are having *warranty work* performed. An unscrupulous dealer may argue that you brought the car in for another reason, and therefore, he or she is not liable for replacing your car. Many states require that the defects prevent you from using the car for thirty days or more in total, or that the dealer has made four attempts to fix the vehicle. The only way you will prove your case is to have good records.

You must keep careful records of the dates of the problems and repair attempts. Each time the car is taken to the mechanic, record the reason for the visit and the date of the visit. Keep all paperwork you are given and be sure to read it, along with the warranties and guarantees. Try to avoid paying cash. Charge repairs on your credit card so you have some recourse if the repairs are not made properly. You can ask the credit card company to refuse to pay the repair shop until you are satisfied with the job.

ODOMETER FRAUD

The United States Department of Transportation's National Highway Traffic Safety Administration estimates that more than half of all vehicles sold by leasing companies have *odometer tampering.* Leasing companies often turn back the odometer on a high-mileage, late model car to defraud the consumer into believing that the vehicle has much lower mileage. The consumer then purchases a vehicle that is not worth the purchase price. The titles to these cars are often transferred from state to state in order to make the history of the car harder to trace for the buyer.

Most often, a car with high mileage has more repair problems than a car with lower mileage. The unwary buyer will spend more for repairs than he or she would expect. The car might not even run at all, making it almost worthless. The dealer commits fraud when he or she misrepresents the value and nature of the car. It is important for a buyer to do his or her homework before purchasing a vehicle.

Never buy a used car without first having your mechanic inspect the car on his or her premises. The *vehicle identification number* (VIN) should be traced through an Internet service. The dealer should reveal whether the car has been in an accident, flood, or fire, and whether it has been rebuilt—ask these specific questions. A search of the VIN will reveal the car's history for any accidents, plus its accurate mileage.

Be alert if you see that the title is from out of state. Have your mechanic check your car to determine if the wear and tear is consistent with the miles reported by the seller. Check the accuracy of the odometer reading for free at the Carfax website at **www.carfax.com**. You will need to have the seventeen-character vehicle identification number in order to run this odometer check. The VIN is located on the dashboard.

If the mileage is much higher than represented to you, then you have the proof you need to return the car for the purchase price. Contact the dealer as soon as you know that the odometer was reset. You have the common law right to rescind a contract entered into because of the fraud by the dealer. A *rescission* of the sale means that you are canceling the entire sale with the dealer. You are erasing the transaction, as if it had never occurred. Rescission is a remedy for fraud in the inducement of a contract. In other words, the dealer's representation that the car had fewer miles induced you to purchase the car. You would not have paid the same price for a car with 150,000 miles as you would for a car with 50,000 miles.

Contact the dealer and try to resolve the problem. Document your visit and send your letters by certified mail. Take another person with you if you visit the dealer. You will have another witness to verify your account of the odometer trouble. If the dealer is unwilling to refund your money, then you should contact the dealer's corporate offices. Start by contacting the zone customer service office. Next, contact the customer service department at corporate headquarters. If this is not helpful, then contact the legal office or the general counsel's office. (Lawyers take fraud very seriously.)

If you purchased your car with a false odometer reading at a dealer affiliated with a well-known brand—such as Ford, Chrysler, General Motors, Saab, Toyota, Subaru, or Mitsubishi—then you have more alternatives for relief. Automobile manufacturers do not want bad publicity, especially of this type. It can and should require the errant dealer to refund your money. The manufacturer is liable for the acts of the dealer, because the dealer is the agent of the manufacturer.

In addition, odometer tampering constitutes civil and criminal fraud in most states. You can sue for your money back plus damages in civil court, and possibly send the perpetrator to jail. However, be careful in trying to collect your money. You cannot threaten someone with jail in order to collect a debt. File a criminal complaint with your local prosecutor if you have problems collecting your debt.

CONSUMER PROTECTION

Consumer protection agencies have pamphlets for potential buyers that contain helpful advice to avoid dealer fraud. Buyers who finance the purchase or lease of their vehicles should also read consumer finance advice from one of these agencies. For example, a common car dealer scam is to have the consumer sign a blank finance contract, promising to fill in the agreed-upon terms later. The dealer then inserts higher rates and a higher price unbeknownst to the buyer. *Never sign a blank contract.*

There are consumer protection lawyers who will review your case if you have been overcharged or defrauded by a car dealer. Call your local bar association for referrals. The lawyer may not charge a fee if he or she takes your case, as some types of cases require the car dealer or finance company to pay your legal fees and costs.

State consumer watchdog organizations, such as the state attorney general, may sue the dealer on your behalf. There may be a *class action suit* for particularly outrageous dealer behavior. (This is a lawsuit in which one person sues on behalf of all others who have the same problem.)

The *Better Business Bureau* (BBB) operates an arbitration service for car dealer complaints. Check your local chapter for details. This is a voluntary out-of-court forum for resolving your complaint. A third party (the arbitrator) hears from the car dealer and you (the owner). The arbitrator's decision is enforceable if the consumer accepts the decision. The car dealer must obey the ruling.

INSURANCE

What happens if your insurance company refuses to pay your claim after an accident? Do you have any recourse? This chapter cannot cover all aspects of vehicles and insurance, but there is enough guidance here to enable you to be a more informed consumer.

Each state regulates the sale of insurance. The state authorities can revoke the license of an insurance company or agent that does not pay legitimate claims. There are substandard insurance companies that make a practice of routinely rejecting claims for automobile accidents. (*Substandard* companies specialize in selling insurance to drivers with poor records.) They hope that if they reject your legitimate claim often enough, you will give up. Do not let them get away with this! Complain to the state authorities. These companies generate many complaints from consumers for failure to pay claims.

There are many insurance companies that are very helpful in processing claims. Your own insurance company may help you collect the claim through the process of *subrogation*. In this process, your vehicle is repaired by your company even though the other driver is at fault, and in return, you agree to assign your right to collect damages from the other driver's insurance company. Then, the other driver's company will be liable for the cost. Ask your insurance agent for information. Always report an accident to your own insurance company immediately.

Insurance companies like to replace the damaged parts of your car with generic parts. These parts may not be of high quality, and they may not meet the specifications of your car's manufacturer. At least forty states have laws regulating the use of generic parts by insurance companies. Know your rights. If an insurer is using generic parts, be sure the parts meet quality standards.

FINANCING

Federal and state laws regulate the extension of consumer credit. The terms of the loan, including *annual percentage rate* (APR), monthly payment, and length (term) of the loan, must be disclosed on the face of the loan documents. If you believe that you have been preyed upon, consult your state's attorney general or the agency responsible for enforcing consumer laws in your state.

Also consider consulting a consumer lawyer. These lawyers may not charge for a consultation. Consumer lawyers may not charge you an individual fee, because the creditor must pay their fees if the case is successful. Also, you may be part of a class action suit where the creditor—not you—pays the fees.

The Better Business Bureau in your area may offer mediation and arbitration of car sales disputes. Their website for this kind of problem can be found at **www.dr.bbb.org/autoline**.

CREDIT LIFE INSURANCE

Credit life insurance is sold to buyers who purchase items on credit, such as cars, appliances, and electronics. The insurer promises to make your payments if you are ill and cannot work. These policies rarely make the promised payments, because the policy fine print has so many conditions and exclusions. Credit life insurance is highly profitable for the seller, and is rarely a good buy for the consumer. The premiums are added into the finance price of the sale, thus increasing the amount of money you owe.

TAKING ACTION—STEP-BY-STEP

1. Contact the seller of the vehicle.

2. If you do not receive satisfaction from the seller, contact the regional office of the automobile manufacturer, called the *zone office*. Ask the regional manager to resolve your problem. If this does not solve your problem, go to the corporate headquarters for help. If you have a warranty, check to see if the warranty covers the problem.

3. If you purchased your vehicle from somewhere other than an automobile dealer, send a certified letter to the seller outlining the problem and describing the action you want the seller to take to fix your problem.

4. After about ten business days, if you still have not received any response to your certified letter, contact your local government consumer affairs office (if you live in a large metropolitan area). If you purchased the car from a dealer, contact your state attorney general or the Better Business Bureau.

5. Remember that odometer fraud or selling a wrecked car as new is a crime. You may want to contact the police.

6. Finally, contact an attorney. Lawyers specializing in lemon laws are available in every state. Call your local bar association. Look on the Internet under lemon law attorneys. You may also sue the person or company that sold you the vehicle in small claims court by yourself, if you cannot get a lawyer to take your case.

Letter 2.1:
Lemon Laws—Rescind the Sale

Easy Rider
9851 Redstone Circle
Fort Wayne, IN 29434
555-555-0000

November 17, 2007

Hoosier Friendly Car Dealership
Ms. Linda Larson
General Manager
2764 Highway 100
Fort Wayne, IN 29434

Re: Defective New Car

Dear Ms. Larson:

Please be advised that I purchased a new 2007 automobile, a Capitol Cruiser, from your dealership on November 1, 2007. The car broke down on the way home from your dealership—the day I bought it.

You towed it back to the dealership and promised me it would be repaired by November 15. I picked it up from your showroom over the weekend. The electrical system gave out again on my way home.

You now have the car in your garage for repairs of the same problem for the third time in less than one month. If it is not repaired to my satisfaction this time, I will rescind the sale. A copy of the sales contract is enclosed.

Very truly yours,

Easy Rider

Letter 2.2:
Lemon Laws—Replacement of Vehicle

Easy Rider
9851 Redstone Circle
Fort Wayne, IN 29434
555-555-0000

November 17, 2007

Hoosier Friendly Car Dealership
Ms. Linda Larson
General Manager
2764 Highway 100
Fort Wayne, IN 29434

Re: Defective New Car

Dear Ms. Larson:

I am writing to inform you that the new car I purchased from you on November 1, 2007, still does not work, despite your best efforts to repair the car. Once again, the electrical system failed and the car died as soon as I drove more than a few feet. The car was towed to your dealership.

This is the last chance I am giving you to fix the car. If the car does not function as a new car should—flawlessly—then I shall expect to have this car replaced with a brand-new Cruiser. I also request reimbursement for the cost of a rental car I had to use because my new car does not work. A copy of the bill for the rental is enclosed.

Very truly yours,

Easy Rider

Letter 2.3:
Defective New Car—
Request for Better Business Bureau Arbitration

Unhappy Owner
1 Desert Way
La Quinta, CA 73106
222-344-0001

June 13, 2007

Better Business Bureau Auto Line
4200 Wilson Boulevard
Suite 800
Arlington, VA 22203

Re: New Car Warranty

Dear Sir or Madam:

I am filing a complaint about the new car I purchased from the Maxwell Motor Company in May 2007. The electrical system failed after 1,000 miles. The air conditioning has not worked correctly since I drove it out of the showroom.

I have taken the car for service at the Maxwell dealership, but the problems have not been fixed. Please resolve this problem through your arbitration program. I understand that this is offered at no cost to the customer.

Very truly yours,

Unhappy Owner

Letter 2.4:
Odometer Fraud on Used Car

Gullible Buyer
220 Arlington Road
Very Cold, MN 30167
333-255-5555

June 20, 2007

Mr. Bill Conniver, Owner
Viking Motors
800 Norse Boulevard
Very Cold, MN 30167

Re: Odometer Fraud

Dear Mr. Conniver:

I am writing concerning the used car I purchased from your dealership on June 8. Your salesman told me the car was lightly used, having only 24,800 miles on it. The odometer reading was 24,800. Once I drove the car home, it had many problems.

I took the car to my mechanic. He advised me that the car had a lot of miles and had been fixed after an accident. I checked the VIN history and learned that the car has closer to 80,000 miles on it. The car had been in an accident and rebuilt—a fact that was not disclosed to me.

I am rescinding the purchase of this car. Your salesperson misrepresented a material fact that I relied on in deciding to purchase the car.

Please call me to discuss the arrangements for the return of the car and for the refund of my purchase price of $18,000.

Very truly yours,

Gullible Buyer

Letter 2.5:
Odometer Fraud;
Second Letter to Dealership

Gullible Buyer
220 Arlington Road
Very Cold, MN 30167
333-255-5555

June 27, 2007

Mr. Bill Conniver, Owner
Viking Motors
800 Norse Boulevard
Very Cold, MN 30167

Re: Odometer Fraud

Dear Mr. Conniver:

I have not heard from you concerning the rescission of the purchase of my car.

The car will be returned to you on July 1, 2007, at 9 a.m. Unless I receive a cashier's check for the full amount of my purchase price of $18,000, I shall take legal action immediately.

Very truly yours,

Gullible Buyer

Letter 2.6:
Odometer Fraud;
Follow-Up to Manufacturer

Gullible Buyer
220 Arlington Road
Very Cold, MN 30167
333-255-5555

July 1, 2007

Customer Service Department
Spectacular Automobile Manufacturing Company
99 Roadster Boulevard
Detroit, MI 44098

Re: Viking Motors Odometer Fraud

Dear Sir or Madam:

Please be advised that I purchased a car from your dealer, Viking Motors. I found after the purchase that the odometer had been turned back from about 80,000 miles to 24,800 miles. Enclosed are copies of my correspondence with the dealership trying to return the car and to receive a refund of my purchase price. The dealer has not responded. The manager at the dealership refused to accept the car when I tried to return it this morning.

Unless I receive a refund of my purchase price of $18,000 within seven days, I shall have no choice but to pursue my legal remedies. I am prepared to return the car at any time you direct. It is currently in my garage.

Very truly yours,

Gullible Buyer

Letter 2.7:
Insurance Claim—
Repairs Made with Used Parts

Michael Motorist
88 Seashell Drive
Savannah, GA 05347
555-555-1255

October 2, 2007

Pilgrim Insurance Company
33 Beacon Street
Boston, MA 23767

Re: Policy #L-550896

Dear Sir or Madam:

On May 15, 2007, my car was hit by another automobile making an illegal left turn. You advised me to take the car to your collision repair center. I followed your instructions and had the car repaired there. Many parts needed to be replaced. A copy of the repair invoice is enclosed.

Shortly after I picked up my repaired car, I noticed problems in performance. I took the car back to your collision center, but was told there was nothing wrong. I took the car to my own mechanic. He advised me that used parts were placed in my car during the repair process.

I expect to have new, brand-name parts used to repair my car. It should be returned to the state it was in before the accident. Please advise when I may return the car to you for these repairs.

Very truly yours,

Michael Motorist

Letter 2.8:
Insurance Claim—Nonpayment;
Follow-Up to Insurance Company

Robert Rider
12 Bonnie Glen Court
Pasadena, CA 91222
555-555-1010

April 12, 2007

Substandard Insurance Company
90 Weasel Way
Claremont, CA 91444

Re: Claim #00446581

Dear Sir or Madam:

On March 1, 2007, your insured, Careless Connors, ran a red light and collided with my car. A police officer witnessed the accident. Mr. Connors received a ticket. The court date was April 2. The judge found him guilty on all counts. A copy of the judgment is enclosed.

I submitted a claim to you on March 5. You have not made any attempt to pay this claim for damage to my car for the sum of $1,200. A copy of the bill is enclosed.

I expect you to remit a check for $1,200 to me immediately. If I do not receive a check promptly, I will file a complaint with the state insurance commission. I will also consider taking legal action.

Very truly yours,

Robert Rider

Letter 2.9:
Complaint to Dealer Regarding
Hybrid Vehicle Repair Service

Joe Treehugger
40 Ecology Drive
Evergreen, WA 31245
444-333-2121

May 5, 2007

Mr. High Volume, Owner
Local Dealership
Car Dealer Row
Evergreen, WA 31232

Re: Hybrid Car Repairs

Dear Mr. Volume:

I am writing to express my disappointment with the long time it took your service department to repair my 2007 hybrid car. It was damaged in a car accident. The parts were not available for over six weeks. The mechanics were not familiar with the car, even though I purchased it at your dealership. If you sell these wonderful hybrid cars, you should be able to service them.

I cannot recommend you to my friends if this is the kind of service you provided.

Very truly yours,

Joe Treehugger

Letter 2.10:
Credit Life Insurance
Assessed on Car Loan

Sam Smith
180 South Hubbard Street
Chicago, IL 60601
773-555-5555

October 13, 2007

Jack Brown, Owner
Friendly Jack Cars
6700 North Western Avenue
Chicago, IL 60626

Re: Refund of Sales Charges

Dear Mr. Brown:

On June 5, 2007, I bought a new Asta sports utility vehicle from you. Your salesperson charged me $375 for credit life insurance. He stated that credit life insurance was required when financing a car.

Please refund the $375 to me and recalculate the loan charges. I now understand that federal law prohibits this charge. The Truth in Lending Act specifically prohibits requiring the sale of credit life insurance in order to secure financing.

I trust that this is an oversight by an uninformed sales person. I expect the revised loan and my check within five (5) business days. A copy of my sales contract is enclosed.

Very truly yours,

Sam Smith

3
Computers

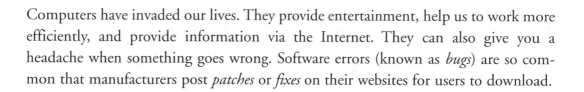

Computers have invaded our lives. They provide entertainment, help us to work more efficiently, and provide information via the Internet. They can also give you a headache when something goes wrong. Software errors (known as *bugs*) are so common that manufacturers post *patches* or *fixes* on their websites for users to download.

Email has been a significant part of the invasion—and the headache. Whether you are addicted to your personal messaging telephone/Internet access device, or you depend on email for business or to keep in touch with relatives, email is a 21st century necessity. The email experience has been fouled by thieves, con artists, sales pitches, predators, pornography purveyors, spammers, and others who attempt to impose their unwanted attentions on us.

Most of us rely on our computers for business and personal use. Having computer access is a necessary part of life. When buying a computer, always buy a product with a warranty, and keep copies of your sales receipts and warranties. These are very important pieces of paper to protect your rights.

DEFECTIVE COMPUTER MERCHANDISE

Printers and scanners may refuse to cooperate with the computer, software may not perform as promised, and hardware may fail. Do not spend too much time trying to get your computer to work. Most likely, the machine has defective chips or other technical problems. Send it back for another machine or a credit if you cannot get it up and running.

Many of the companies that manufacture these items do not provide a number for customer service. If they do provide customer service, the companies may first ask for your credit card—they have the nerve to charge you for trying to get their defective products to work! Federal and state law may offer some help, depending on the problem.

Make certain you shop at a reputable store with a return policy that permits you to return a computer or software once the box or seal is opened. Some stores will not take back software if the box has been opened.

It cannot be repeated too often—do not pay cash for your purchase. *Always* purchase computers and related items with your credit card. If the product does not work, you can explain the problem to your credit card company and dispute the charge. You will not have to pay the bill if the dispute is resolved in your favor. This gives you some leverage to get the manufacturer to replace the product.

INTERNET SERVICE

Internet service providers are a source of frustration for many users. Security is sometimes lax, allowing hackers to get into the networks and retrieve personal information.

High-speed Internet connection services are growing rapidly. Digital subscriber line (DSL) is a term the telephone companies have given to broadband digital services that are provided over existing telephone lines. The competition in this consumer market sector is the high-speed digital service provided by the cable companies over the existing cable lines. Both provide Internet service to your home. Their software may be defective or incompatible with your current computer equipment. Some DSL providers also charge several hundred dollars to connect your equipment to the high-speed link.

Look on the Internet for a help page for your service. You may be able to email a company technician with your problem or call for advice. They make it very difficult for you register a complaint online or to cancel their service. Finding a telephone number to speak with a customer service representative can be quite a challenge. Likewise, it is hard to find an address for communicating by U.S. mail.

If all else fails, if a company is publicly traded, the *Securities and Exchange Commission* (SEC) requires reports that must be filed periodically. The address, telephone numbers, and names of executives are listed in these documents. You can find these on the Internet by typing the name of the company and "SEC filings" into a search engine on the Internet.

INTERNET CRIMES

It is a federal crime to commit certain fraudulent and dishonest acts on a computer or using a computer system. The Department of Justice maintains a website tracking crimes, laws, and other useful information at **www.cybercrime.gov**.

Many states are passing laws to criminalize acts committed in cyberspace. Typical subjects include stalking, adults preying on children, child pornography, and hacking or unauthorized use of a computer system or account. As thieves increase their activities in cyberspace, authorities will extend their reach to protect the consumer's rights.

Never put personal information on an unsecure site. Theft may occur even on a supposedly secure site. Identity theft is a nightmare for anyone caught in this Hitchcock-like dilemma. Your bank accounts can be cleaned out with a few keystrokes.

ONLINE PURCHASES

Never pay cash for an online purchase. Always put such purchases on a credit card, not a debit card. This way, you have some recourse if the item is not shipped or is defective. Your credit card should not be charged until the item is shipped, but some sellers will charge your card once the order is entered.

According to the Federal Trade Commission (FTC), an Internet vendor is required to ship an order within the time promised on its website or no later than thirty days after the order is placed. If the shipment cannot be sent on time, the vendor is required to notify you of the delay. It must estimate when the product will be sent and ask for your approval of the delayed shipment. You can refuse the extended shipping time, which would cancel your order. Today, many companies have identification numbers for each order that enable you to track the location of your purchase.

If your purchase does not come as promised, do not wait to contact the seller. You may file a complaint with the FTC online at **www.ftc.gov**.

SPAM

Is there anyone online today who has not received unsolicited email from vendors who want to sell something? Subscriptions, vacations, cars, dubious drugs, Canadian prescription services, and movie tickets are just a few of the subjects of these unwanted messages. *Spam* is unsolicited commercial junk email. These unwanted messages clog our computers at work and at home with offers to help us enhance our sex lives, become millionaires, buy wonder vitamins, receive free movie tickets or other free gifts, and other nuisance items.

The FTC has estimated that 86% of addresses posted to websites and to newsgroups receive spam, and that 50% of addresses posted on free personal websites receive spam. Internet providers are trying to filter the unwanted commercial emails, but many emails still get through.

Congress enacted a law to prevent unwanted commercial messages through email, known as the *CAN-SPAM Act of 2003*. This acronym stands for *Controlling the Assault of Non-Solicited Pornography and Marketing Act*. The Act prohibits a sender of email from disguising its address, or using a false name or address to send email for commercial purposes. It is also illegal to harvest the names of users who have contacted websites when the owner of the site assures the email sender of privacy. The law makes it illegal to send sexually explicit messages without a warning message, thus providing protection to email recipients attacked by frequent and unsolicited sexual messages. The CAN-SPAM Act of 2003 contains the following main points, as outlined by the Federal Trade Commission.

- It bans false or misleading header information. The email's "From," "To," and routing information—including the originating domain name and email address—must be accurate and identify the person who initiated the email.

- It prohibits deceptive subject lines. The subject line cannot mislead the recipient about the contents or subject matter of the message.

- It requires that commercial senders of email give recipients an opt-out method.

- It requires that commercial email be identified as an advertisement and include the sender's valid physical postal address.

The penalty for failure to comply with the law is $11,000 per violation. There may be additional penalties for deceptive and misleading advertising conduct. There may also be criminal penalties under the CAN-SPAM Act when a commercial sender tries to evade this law by using phony email addresses, disguising the sender's address, using another computer or email account to send unwanted commercial messages without permission of the owner, or using fake domain names to hide the sender's true identity.

Your computer could be hijacked by commercial senders violating the Act by disguising their messages sent to millions of people in a process called *spam zombies*. This problem is so prevalent that the FTC has devoted team resources to root out this cyber problem. For more information, visit the FTC's website on the subject at **www.ftc.gov/ bcp/conline/edcams/spam/zombie**.

In addition to the CAN-SPAM Act, all states have passed their own legislation to outlaw unwanted commercial messages sent through cyberspace, except the following.

- Alabama
- Hawaii
- Kentucky
- Massachusetts
- Mississippi
- Montana

- Nebraska
- New Hampshire
- New Jersey
- New York
- South Carolina
- Vermont

Check the law in your state for more details.

If you have received spam, complain about it. Send it to your local law enforcement authorities. The Federal Trade Commission has been very active in pursuing violations of the CAN-SPAM Act. The FTC has a website for spam at **www.ftc.gov/spam**. The site has a thorough discussion of spam for consumers and for businesses. You may file a complaint about receiving unwanted commercial email messages by emailing **spam@uce.gov**. Include the full header of the unwanted message in your complaint.

Another website with useful information about laws regulating spam is located at **http://law.spamcon.org**.

You should complain to your Internet service provider as well as to the FTC. Internet service providers should have junk mail and spam filters installed to prevent these unwanted messages. You should also install your own security software to block spam.

TAKING ACTION—STEP-BY-STEP

1. Call the customer service number for help if your computer does not work. You may not be setting the computer up correctly. Have the representative guide you through the process. If you cannot get a human being on the telephone, or if the manufacturer charges you for this information, ask a tech-savvy friend to come over to help you get the computer up and running.

    NOTE: *Be aware that the customer service representative will often tell you to reinstall the operating system. That is not a very helpful suggestion. Most consumers do not have the ability to run the diagnostic tools shipped with the computer. Some of these customer service centers are there to provide a mere façade of service.*

2. If you still cannot get the machine to work, return it to the seller. If you followed the advice in this chapter and charged the purchase on your personal credit card, you can contact the credit card company and refuse to pay the bill. Notify the credit card company that you have returned it to the seller and are disputing the charge.

    If you ordered the computer from an online vendor or a catalog company, be sure to obtain an authorization number from the seller before you ship your equipment back. The seller may try to avoid giving you this number. Document any such problems.

3. If the seller refuses to take the product back, document the reason. Write down what the seller tells you. If possible, ask a manager to write down the reason you cannot return the product. The store has the right to refuse a return if you did not follow its return policies, such as waiting too long before you return the computer. That being said, many sellers will still take back a defective computer, because they do not want unhappy customers.

    Computers purchased online or from a catalog should be shipped within thirty days or less. If the item is not in stock, you must receive a message from the seller telling you that it is not available and asking if you wish to cancel the purchase. The seller must tell you when it expects to receive the out-of-stock computer. If your computer does not arrive, then call and write the seller. Refuse to pay your credit card bill if the seller billed your card and you have not received the product.

4. Complain to the consumer agency in the seller's state and to your local consumer affairs organization. Remember that your state attorney general has a consumer affairs division. Many states allow you to file complaints online. The Better Business Bureau is a private agency offering dispute resolution. It also has a list of businesses that have many consumer complaints. Complain to the Federal Trade Commission if your merchandise does not arrive.

NOTE: *Software presents a different problem that is far worse than the hardware situation. The consumer has very few rights under the seller's shrink-wrap license. The retailer may disavow responsibility once you open the package.*

Letter 3.1:
Defective Computer

Dissatisfied Buyer
18 Grand Street
Cheyenne, WY 09321
888-222-0000

August 2, 2007

Horizon Computer Company
1324 Main Avenue
St. Paul, MN 43422

Re: Defective Computer

Dear Sir or Madam:

Please be advised that I recently purchased a new Horizon Ace computer from your website. It cost $2,500. The computer arrived on July 31. It does not work.

I am very experienced working with computers, and still had to call your customer service department for advice, which was not helpful. I read the manual and tried all the suggestions. I believe that this machine has a defective chip.

I am returning the machine to you by commercial shipment. Please credit my Visa account immediately. A copy of the bill is enclosed.

Very truly yours,

Dissatisfied Buyer

Letter 3.2:
Defective Merchandise—
Computer Incompatibility

Barbara Black
813 Locust Way
Madison, WI 23490
555-555-5500

May 3, 2007

Big Banana Computers
309 Main Street
Madison, WI 23490

Re: Computer Compatibility

Dear Sir or Madam:

I purchased a Big Banana computer, Model #5698, at your store on April 30. The sales literature states that it is compatible with any printer, including the one I already own.

I have tried to get your computer to work with my existing hardware. It will not. I determined that I had to invest in costly software before your machine would run with my printer.

You should reimburse me for the cost of this software or accept the return of the machine and the software. It does not perform as promised. I have enclosed copies of my receipts for your machine and for the software.

Very truly yours,

Barbara Black

<u>Letter 3.3:</u>
Defective Merchandise—
Incompatible Software

Internet Subscriber
607 Maple Street
Durango, CO 20202
555-555-5555

May 1, 2007

Customer Service Department
Wild West DSL Provider
P.O. Box 901
Durango, CO 20202

Re: Faulty DSL Software

Dear Sir or Madam:

On April 16, I agreed to one year of DSL service. You sent me the kit to install this service myself. I am an experienced computer engineer; however, I cannot install your software because it is defective and incompatible with the computer I have. When I signed up for your service, I discussed the type of computer I had with your representative.

I called your technical support line for help several times. Your staff informed me that there are many problems like the ones I described.

Please send me new software for my Ace Zip Computers system. I will not pay the bill for my account (#19054) until the service is operable.

Very truly yours,

Internet Subscriber

Letter 3.4:
Internet Service—
Lack of Security

Frustrated Subscriber
11 Big Street
Austin, TX 00000
310-289-4588

June 8, 2007

Subscriber Services
Wired America Company
75 Skyscraper Place
New York, NY 10009

Re: Hacked Account Complaint

Dear Sir or Madam:

Please be advised that my Internet account was hacked by an intruder on June 7. I learned of the problem when I tried to access my account that afternoon. I called your customer service number and was told that I could not receive any information because my address was not the address on the account.

This is absurd! The hacker inserted his information for mine. You are trying to verify my account identity with stolen information. Your representative refused to check the billing address previously used or other information that would have correctly identified me. The solution suggested by your representative was to open a new account.

This is the second time within a year that my account has been hacked. Our credit card information was jeopardized on your site. This is also the second time I had to cancel all my credit cards.

Please investigate and correct this problem immediately.

Very truly yours,

Frustrated Subscriber

Letter 3.5:
Internet Crime—
Stolen Information

Susan Sprocket
25 Sleepy Hollow Drive
New Buffalo, NY 02345
555-555-5555

January 3, 2007

Manager
All Night Copy Shop
Local College
New Buffalo, NY 02345

Re: Stolen Financial Information

Dear Sir or Madam:

On December 2, 2006, I rented time at a computer station in your store. During that time, I shopped online for holiday gifts. Shortly after I provided my financial information at your computer, I learned that unauthorized charges were made to my American Express account.

I have asked American Express to investigate this matter. At this time, it is believed that someone gained unlawful access to your computer system, and stole my information.

Please contact the police to report this cybercrime. I am sure many other people in your shop were affected, too. Enclosed are the unauthorized charges.

Very truly yours,

Susan Sprocket

Letter 3.6:
Spam

George Anderson
99 Bosworth Avenue
Durham, NC 23000
322-555-1111

May 20, 2007

President
Ace Internet Company
2200 Skyscraper Street
New York, NY 20103

Re: Spam

Dear Sir or Madam:

I have subscribed to your Internet service for two years. During that time, the amount of spam I have received has increased tremendously. The pop-up ads are particularly annoying, and the content of the spam emails is very offensive.

Please explain the measures you are taking to filter these offensive and irritating messages. For $30 a month, I expect you to take care of the customer. There are other Internet services vying for my account. I will consider switching providers unless this problem is resolved.

Very truly yours,

George Anderson

Letter 3.7:
Internet Service Provider—
Spam Problem

I.M. Connected
3085 Internet Highway
Silicon Valley, CA 91203
714-348-9521

May 1, 2007

Internet Service Provider
1200 Green Street
St. Louis, MO 63188

Re: Spam Complaint

Dear Sir or Madam:

I am writing to complain about the vast quantity of vile spam I receive in my email account with you. Although I have complained numerous times online, you have failed to respond to my concerns. The spam is as troublesome as ever.

If you cannot filter the unwanted and offensive email, then I shall be forced to switch to a provider that can.

Thank you for your prompt attention to this matter.

Very truly yours,

I.M. Connected

Letter 3.8:
Internet Service Provider—Cancel Service; Second Letter

I.M. Connected
3085 Internet Highway
Silicon Valley, CA 91203
714-348-9521

May 15, 2007

Internet Service Provider
1200 Green Street
St. Louis, MO 63188

Re: Spam Complaint

Dear Sir or Madam:

On May 1, 2007, I wrote via U.S. mail notifying you of my dissatisfaction with the spam I receive in my email account. The sheer quantity of advertising and pornographic messages clogs my email. I am required to spend hours each week erasing and blocking the unwanted messages.

Once again, you have ignored my requests to contact me to discuss a resolution to the spam attacks. As a result, I am canceling my subscription immediately. I am switching my Internet Service Provider to a company that uses filtering software to block the spam.

Very truly yours,

I.M. Connected

Letter 3.9:
Spam—
Violating State Law

Mary Morgan
900 West Robin Hood Lane
Little Rock, AR 20301
555-555-5555

July 10, 2007

Ridiculous Promises Company
P.O. Box 88
Goofy, CA 91220

Re: Spam

Dear Sir or Madam:

I am a subscriber to Acme Internet Provider. Your company sends me at least five unwanted emails daily. These communications are lewd, and they violate Arkansas law and general good taste.

Arkansas law requires all commercial and sexually suggestive email to be clearly labeled as "ADV-ADULT" in the subject identification line. You must have a functioning email reply and an opt-out method. You must honor the opt-out requests.

Do not send me any more messages.

Very truly yours,

Mary Morgan

Letter 3.10:
Internet Advertiser—
Delete Name from Email List

I.M. Connected
3085 Internet Highway
Silicon Valley, CA 91203
714-348-9521

May 5, 2007

Obnoxious Advertiser
890 Commercial Avenue
Orlando, FL 23904

Re: Spam Complaint

Dear Sir or Madam:

Please delete my name from your email list: imconnected@coolmail.com.
I have already made this request online several times without result. I
no longer want to receive any communication from you. If you fail to
remove my name from your list, I will have no choice but to file a formal complaint with the Federal Trade Commission.

Thank you,

I.M. Connected

Letter 3.11:
FTC—Internet Advertiser Refuses to Remove Name from List

I.M. Connected
3085 Internet Highway
Silicon Valley, CA 91203
714-348-9521

May 20, 2007

Federal Trade Commission
600 Pennsylvania Avenue, NW
Washington, DC 20580

Re: Spam

Dear Sir or Madam:

I am writing to complain that the Obnoxious Advertiser has failed and refused to remove my name from its online subscription list, despite numerous requests. Enclosed please find my complaint form printed from your Internet consumer site.

Please require the company to remove my name.

Very truly yours,

I.M. Connected

Letter 3.12:
Online Purchase—
Shipment Not Received

Dissatisfied Buyer
18 Grand Street
Cheyenne, WY 09321
888-222-0000

August 12, 2007

Horizon Computer Company
1324 Main Avenue
St. Paul, MN 43422

Re: Failure to Ship Computer

Dear Sir or Madam:

On July 31, 2007, I purchased a Horizon Ace computer from your Internet site. The price is $2,500. To date, I have not received notice of shipment or the computer.

I have called your website customer service number without result.

Please advise when the computer was shipped or will be shipped. A copy of my invoice is enclosed.

Very truly yours,

Dissatisfied Buyer

Letter 3.13:
Online Purchase;
Second Letter

Dissatisfied Buyer
18 Grand Street
Cheyenne, WY 09321
888-222-0000

September 5, 2007

Horizon Computer Company
1324 Main Avenue
St. Paul, MN 43422

Re: Failure to Ship Computer

Dear Sir or Madam:

I purchased a Horizon Ace computer from your website for $2,500 on July 31, 2007. Despite telephone calls and correspondence to you inquiring about the shipment of the computer, I have not received any information concerning the computer.

Please advise when the computer was shipped and when it will be delivered. A copy of my invoice is enclosed.

Unless I hear from you or receive the computer within ten days, I will cancel the order.

Very truly yours,

Dissatisfied Buyer

4
Employment

Both federal and state laws protect your rights in the workplace. Sexual harassment and discrimination are prohibited. Discrimination based on age, religion, race, color, sex, or national origin is not permitted. The *Equal Employment Opportunity Commission* (EEOC) is the federal agency that is responsible for regulating and enforcing the many laws prohibiting workplace discrimination. States and cities often have human rights commissions and labor departments that perform similar tasks.

DISCRIMINATION

The main federal law that prohibits discrimination is the *Civil Rights Act of 1964*. Under the Act, it is unlawful for an employer to discriminate against any individual in matters of hiring, firing, compensation, terms, conditions, or privileges of employment because of the individual's race, color, religion, sex, or national origin. The Act requires employers to treat members of the opposite sex equally, treat employees of different races equally, and to reasonably accommodate the religious needs of employees.

Legal advice may be available from nonprofit groups such as the National Organization for Women (NOW), the Anti-Defamation League, the American Association of Retired Persons (AARP), the National Association for the Advancement of Colored People (NAACP), and from your local bar association. If you are a member of a union, you should contact your union for assistance.

You may also contact the Equal Employment Opportunity Commission or your state labor department for help. The EEOC website has a link for filing a complaint at **www.eeoc.gov**. You may also contact EEOC headquarters at:

U.S. Equal Employment Opportunity Commission
1801 L Street, NW
Washington, DC 20507
202-663-4900

In any case, be aware that the time for filing a complaint or lawsuit is very specific. If you miss the deadline for filing, you will lose your right to proceed with your complaint. Depending on the type of discrimination you experience and the applicable law, you may have no more than 180 days after the discrimination occurs to file a complaint with the EEOC. Hiring an attorney is highly recommended.

This is a complex and constantly evolving area of the law. If you think that your rights have been violated, try to document the discrimination. Get the names of people with whom you spoke and any possible witnesses. You should also consult an attorney immediately.

Mental or Physical Disabilities

Employers with fifteen or more employees are prohibited from discriminating against employees or prospective employees with a known mental or physical disability under the *Americans with Disabilities Act* (ADA). A *Guide to Disability Rights* is available online at **www.usdoj.gov/crt/ada**.

Employers must make reasonable accommodations for disabled workers. A person with a disability has 180 days to file a complaint with the Equal Employment Opportunity Commission if an employer has discriminated against him or her. Complaints must be filed with the correct agency within a strict time limit. It is advisable to consult an attorney to avoid missing a filing deadline, as this is a very complex area of the law.

Age Discrimination

Federal law prohibits age discrimination under the *Age Discrimination in Employment Act*. Workers 40 years and older are protected from discrimination by this federal law. The law applies to companies with twenty or more employees. The law also applies to government agencies. A website explaining the law is at **www.eeoc.gov/facts/age.html**.

EQUAL PAY

The *Equal Pay Act* is a federal law that prohibits unequal pay for equal work. Local laws may also be available to guarantee this right. Check with your state and city labor commission, attorney general, and civil rights offices. The law does not require you to file a complaint with the Equal Employment Opportunity Commission before filing a lawsuit.

SEXUAL HARASSMENT

Sexual harassment is against the law. Actions of sexual harassment include, but are not limited to: placing suggestive pictures in a locker; making lewd comments or gestures; touching or threatening to touch another person in a sexual or threatening way; making sexual advances; and, leaving pornographic pictures in a locker room. If an abusive workplace is created by these actions, then this most likely constitutes sexual harassment. The law used by those filing cases of sexual harassment is usually Title VII of the Civil Rights Act of 1964. The Equal Employment Opportunity Commission (EEOC), a federal agency, has a website with information about the laws against sexual harassment at **www.eeoc.gov/types/sexual_harassment.html**.

Complaints can be filed by either males or females. The EEOC reports that in 2005, 14.3% of complaints were filed by males. The offensive behavior is against the law even if the victim does not complain. Anyone offended by the behavior can complain.

Litigation is not the only alternative for those victimized by sexual harassment. The EEOC offers free mediation to resolve differences between employer and employee.

Both parties must agree to participate. This free mediation service is also offered to all persons with type of harassment complaint. The EEOC website for mediation is **www.eeoc.gov/mediate/index.html**.

FAMILY AND MEDICAL LEAVE ACT

Generally, the *Family and Medical Leave Act* (FMLA) is a federal law that requires employers to give eligible employees twelve weeks of unpaid leave to attend to family issues, such as the birth of a child, adoption of a child, and family illness. An employee may also use this law to take time off for his or her own serious illness.

The law describes certain requirements for the employee to be entitled to this leave. For example, your employer must have fifty or more employees within seventy-five miles of the worksite. You, the employee, must have worked at least 1,250 hours for the employer. For nonemergency leave requests, you must notify your employer at least thirty days in advance of the time you wish to take your leave. You are entitled to have your benefits maintained during your leave, but you must pay for them.

EMPLOYEE RECORDS

Thirty-nine states allow employees to view their personnel records. The state laws vary widely, from free access in California to limited access of only medical records in Ohio. Illinois has a very liberal policy that allows employees to place a response in their files to evaluations. Many states require only public employers to provide access to personnel files.

If possible under your state law, you should periodically review your file. There could be negative information in there that could hurt you. There could also be incorrect information in there that could prevent you from being promoted. Correct the records if your state allows this remedy. Contact your state's Department of Labor for more information about the specific laws of your area.

MEMBERS OF THE MILITARY

Today, many men and women have been called to active duty for military service. Others have been called for disaster assistance because of the horrific hurricanes, floods, and tornadoes we have experienced. Unfortunately, many employers of these individuals are not following the laws designed to protect their jobs while they are serving their country. Too many members of our military have returned from service to find that their jobs are gone and that their health benefits are not honored. There are federal and state laws in force to protect these veterans of military service.

All employees (except, by definition, independent contractors) are covered by the far-reaching *Uniformed Services Employment and Re-employment Rights Act of 1994* (USERRA), a federal law enacted to protect the job rights of military reserves members, National Guard members, and others called to active duty. This law also prohibits job discrimination against veterans. Rules interpreting this law became effective January 18, 2006.

Under this law, employers must:

- offer a job to employees returning from active duty within two weeks after they apply;

- grant the same seniority the employee would have absent military duty;

- accommodate any disability the veteran may have acquired as a result of service, so long as the veteran is able to perform the duties of the job;

- provide health insurance coverage for the first thirty days after deployment, and offer COBRA continuation of insurance coverage at the expense of the employee after the initial thirty days;

- not treat the employee's military service time as a break in coverage for retirement or pension benefits; and,

- hang a poster stating the USERRA rights of military employees in a prominent place where employees gather.

Employees must follow the guidelines provided by law in notifying their employers about their return to the job. If these rules are not followed, the employee may lose his or her right to return to the same employer at the same job.

Further information is available at **www.dol.gov/ebsa/faqs**. This is the website for the United States Department of Labor for reservists being called to active duty.

TAKING ACTION—STEP-BY-STEP

1. The employee should go to his or her immediate superior to discuss the problem, if this is practical. (If the complaint is about the immediate supervisor, then that is not a good idea.) Discuss the problem in a businesslike manner. Provide written documentation if possible.

2. If the first step does not work, then go to your union representative or the human resources department. File a formal grievance. If you are a union member, then you may receive free legal help at this point. You may wish to consult an attorney.

3. Learn the specific rules for filing a discrimination complaint in your locality. Federal law requires you to file your complaint within a very specific time frame. If you do not follow the law for filing your complaint, you will lose the right to pursue your case.

4. If you choose to file a lawsuit, consult an attorney concentrating in employment law as soon as possible. Before you can file a lawsuit based on sexual, racial, or age discrimination, you must file your complaint with the Equal Employment Opportunities Commission.

    NOTE: *This is a very complex area of law. Your future is at stake. Hire a lawyer if your complaint is not resolved. A lawyer can help you to negotiate a termination package or a settlement of your claim outside of court.*

Letter 4.1:
Racial Discrimination—
Human Resources

Loyal Worker
5792 Collins Avenue
Apartment 222
Miami, FL 40123
555-555-5555

April 5, 2007

Human Resources Manager
Acme Widget Company
94 South Flamingo Street
Miami, FL 40128

Re: Discrimination

Dear Sir or Madam:

On March 28, 2007, I answered your advertisement for factory workers at the main plant. When I arrived to apply for the job, your plant manager refused to give me an application. I asked why he was giving employment applications to others, but not to me. Mr. Snerd, the manager, told me that he had, "bad experiences with my people." He then went on to make several ethnically insulting remarks.

I believe that he refused to give the application to me because I am from India. You should be aware of the discriminatory practices Mr. Snerd has in hiring employees. I have decided to contact you first to determine if you can resolve this matter to my satisfaction.

If this blatant discrimination is not resolved amicably, I will be forced to pursue my legal remedies.

Very truly yours,

Loyal Worker

Letter 4.2:
Religious Discrimination—
Direct Supervisor

Stanley Smith
8040 DeWitt Clinton Parkway
Brooklyn, NY 22222
212-555-5555

July 11, 2007

Assignment Editor
Newsradio Radio Station
2500 Park Avenue
New York, NY 20200

Re: Work Schedule

Dear Editor:

You have scheduled me to work on Saturdays for the month of September. You are new to this station, so you probably do not know that I cannot work Saturdays, the Jewish Sabbath. I cannot work from sundown Friday until after sundown on Saturday. You should also note that I cannot work on Jewish holidays, such as Rosh Hashanah. A list of the holidays and the dates for this year and next is enclosed.

I am available to work other days when my colleagues may prefer not to work. I will be available for work on holidays such as Christmas, Easter, New Year's Eve and Day, plus Sundays. There has never been a problem with this schedule.

You have told me that everyone else at the station works on Saturdays but me. This is because I am the only Orthodox Jewish employee. Federal and local employment discrimination laws guarantee me the right to have my employer respect and accommodate my religious practices.

Very truly yours,

Stanley Smith

Letter 4.3:
Unequal Pay

Rosie Riveter
38 Homefront Avenue
Los Angeles, CA 91333
213-343-5555

May 30, 2007

Personnel Manager
Douglas Aircraft Company
1942 Commercial Boulevard
Los Angeles, CA 91333

Re: Unequal Pay

Dear Sir or Madam:

It has come to my attention that I am paid less than the man next to me on the assembly line. I have worked as a riveter for Douglas Aircraft Company for $12.12 per hour since the day I was hired, November 1, 2006. The man next to me on the assembly line, Roger Reed, was hired on April 1, 2007, at a salary of $15.00 per hour. He has no experience—I trained him.

Please review my file and adjust my pay retroactively. I am sure that this is an oversight on your part.

Thank you,

Rosie Riveter

Letter 4.4:
Accommodations for Disability

Mary Reed
84 Lake Tahoe Road
Lake Tahoe, CA 90433
555-555-5555

July 3, 2007

Molly Manager
Resort Property Management
35 Circle Street
Lake Tahoe, CA 90433

Re: Accommodations for Disability

Dear Ms. Manager:

I am an employee in the accounts receivable department. Recently, I was diagnosed with macular degeneration, a condition that impairs one's eyesight. It can lead to blindness. Right now I am having difficulty seeing the computer screen. There are screens available for visually impaired people.

Please accommodate my visual disability. I can continue doing my job if I have a computer screen that enlarges the images. These are available through our computer vendor, Computer Guys. The cost is comparable to any other good monitor.

Thank you for your cooperation. A letter from my doctor is enclosed.

Very truly yours,

Mary Reed

Letter 4.5:
Failure to Accommodate Disability;
Follow-Up to Manager

Lucille McGillicuddy
623 East 68th Street
New York, NY 10244
212-247-2099

March 11, 2007

Molly Manager
Delicious Chocolate Factory
84 Bleeker Street
New York, NY 20344

Re: Failure to Accommodate Disability

Dear Ms. Manager:

Recently, I broke my leg in an accidental fall at home. My doctor has cleared me to return to work, but I need to use a wheelchair. As you know, I am a candy packer on the assembly line. Standing is customary on the line, but I don't believe there is any reason that would prevent me from working while seated in my wheelchair.

I am asking that you accommodate my disability under the Americans for Disability Act and state law. My supervisor has ignored this request. Please contact me to discuss my return to work.

Very truly yours,

Lucille McGillicuddy

Letter 4.6:
Age Discrimination

Ben Borden
18 Maple Drive
Mayfield, MD 66430
404-262-0099

June 11, 2007

Personnel Manager
Reliable Clock Company
22 Highway 440
Mayfield, MD 66433

Re: Layoff

Dear Sir or Madam:

I have been notified that I am being laid off effective July 1. It concerns me that I am the only person over 40 years of age working at this job, and have now been marked for unemployment.

Employees with far less experience and ability are not being forced to leave. These workers are at least ten years younger than I am. This seems to be age discrimination.

Please contact me to discuss this situation. I prefer to resolve this privately, rather than filing a complaint with a government agency. If necessary, I will take legal action.

Very truly yours,

Ben Borden

Letter 4.7:
Sexual Harassment;
Follow-Up to Human Resources Manager

Mary Doll
88 Drury Lane
Toyland, OR 20044
555-555-0000

March 14, 2007

Human Resources Manager
Ken's Construction Company
90 East Plainfield Road
Toyland, OR 20048

Re: Sexual Harassment

Dear Sir or Madam:

I am writing to notify you that my coworkers at the building site where I am employed as an electrician are sexually harassing me. Past complaints to my supervisor have been to no avail.

Enclosed please find a list of offensive incidents and supporting documentation, including pictures. For example, suggestive notes have been left in my lunchbox, pictures of nude women and men have been posted on the inside and outside of my locker, and many rude remarks have been directed towards me. Some of the men have made sexual advances towards me, even grabbing at me.

I prefer to resolve this privately, but will not hesitate to take legal action if you do not respond within seven days.

Very truly yours,

Mary Doll
Via certified mail

Letter 4.8:
Paternity Leave Request;
Follow-Up to Human Resources

Ward Cleaver
18 Maple Drive
Mayfield, CA 00022
555-555-5555

April 1, 2007

Vice President
Human Resources Department
Mayfield Business Corporation
11 Downtown Office
Mayfield, CA 00022

Re: Family Leave Request

Dear Sir or Madam:

Please be advised that I plan to take paternity leave from May 15 through June 15. My wife expects to give birth to our first child on May 20. Our company personnel manual provides that fathers are entitled to one month of unpaid leave for the birth of a child.

I have advised my manager of this request, but to date have received no confirmation.

Thank you,

Ward Cleaver

Letter 4.9:
Notice to Employers—
Unpaid Family Leave of Absence

Baby Boomer
900 Cass Avenue
Colorado Springs, CO 33058
555-555-1111

July 10, 2007

Human Resources Manager
Colorado Ski Company
P.O. Box 88
Colorado Springs, CO 33058

Re: Request for Leave

Dear Sir or Madam:

Please be advised that I plan to take a family leave of absence for three months commencing September 1 and ending December 1. My elderly mother needs to have both knees replaced. I need to take care of her during this difficult time. I understand that this will be unpaid leave under the Family and Medical Leave Act.

Thank you,

Baby Boomer

Letter 4.10:
Review Employment Record

Edward Employee
518 Crestview Lane
Blue Island, IL 60055
555-555-5555

March 2, 2007

Plant Manager
Big Car Plant
1800 South Busy Street
Industry, IL 60500

Re: Review Employment Record

Dear Sir or Madam:

I am writing to request the opportunity to view my employment records of recent performance reviews. My supervisor refused to give me a copy of the file. I have never requested a chance to see my personnel records before.

Under Illinois law 820 ILCS 40/2 (the Personnel Records Review Act), I have the right to see any information in my employment records. Please contact me to arrange a mutually convenient time for me to review my file.

Very truly yours,

Edward Employee

Letter 4.11:
Employee's Statement to be
Added to Employment Record

Edward Employee
518 Crestview Lane
Blue Island, IL 60055
555-555-5555

March 15, 2007

Plant Manager
Big Car Plant
1800 South Busy Street
Industry, IL 60500

Re: Employment Record

Dear Sir or Madam:

Thank you for providing me the chance to review my personnel file.

I dispute the accuracy of my supervisor's report on my productivity. We discussed this, but could not agree to remove it from the file. Therefore, I am exercising my right to insert my own statement about this report that I believe reflects the situation more accurately. I understand that state law requires you to place the enclosed statement into my employee file.

I am exercising this right pursuant to 820 ILCS 40/6.

Very truly yours,

Edward Employee

Letter 4.12:
Notice to Employer—
Return from Active Duty

G.I. Jane
Army Barracks #10
Any Base, VA 60333

April 23, 2007

Former Employer
3753 Suburban Mall Drive
Suburbia, WV 00312

Re: Return from Active Duty

Dear Mr. Employer:

I am pleased to inform you that my tour of duty with the Army Reserves is coming to an end. My unit will return soon. I will be ready to return to my previous position as human resources manager effective June 1, 2007.

Upon my return, I expect to be reinstated in the same job at the same pay and with the same benefits. I also should not experience any break in my pension or other retirement benefits because of my military duty. My employment rights are protected under the federal USERRA law.

I am looking forward to returning to work.

Very truly yours,

G.I. Jane

5

Finances

In this age of computers and the Internet, the consumer has one more area in which to be wary. Cyberspace contains new frontiers for the dishonest. Your accounts could be wiped out before you even know it. Your identity and money can be stolen with a few keystrokes, using stealth software known as crimeware. *Crimeware* is software stealthily put into your computer, automatic teller machine (ATM), or store payment device. This crimeware may be used to commit various crimes, such as copying and storing your personal information for use by a thief, transmitting your credit card and secure code to a thief's computer, or even copying your trusted bank's website and asking you to verify your passwords and account numbers (also called *scamming*). (Please refer to Chapter 6 in this book for more information about these identity thieves and how to protect yourself.) These new ways to commit theft are in addition to the tried and true methods, such as pickpocketing, purse snatching, and fraud. Always be aware of your finances.

Resolving financial problems often takes several tries. Send letters by certified mail when possible. An alternative method of proving that you mailed a letter is to fill out a *certificate of mailing* at your local post office. This is a small sheet of paper, about the size of an index card, that has the name and address of the sender and the name and address of the recipient. The postal clerk affixes the correct postage and stamps the date of mailing over it. This is proof that you mailed a document. (It is several dollars cheaper than sending letters by certified mail.)

CREDIT CARDS

It is very difficult to function today without a credit card. They can be a great convenience and a necessity in today's e-commerce and mobile society. It is virtually impossible to rent a car or buy an airline ticket online without a credit card in your name. However, when there are billing errors or problems disputing purchases made with the card, the accounting can turn into a nightmare for the consumer.

Many people pay their bills online. Sometimes those payments disappear into the ether, with the credit card issuer claiming to never have received payment. Your bank account was debited with the payment, but the company denies it has been paid. Always print out the confirmation page you receive when paying bills online. Do not lose your confirmation number or transaction number—it will help you prove that you have paid the bill.

Read the slips of paper with the small print from your credit card company, and always read the fine print on your bill. Many credit card companies now require you to submit to arbitration if you have a complaint, and your right to go to court may be limited. This weakens the consumer's rights, but lawmakers have let this happen. If you do not like this, write to your state and federal elected officials. You only have your money and your rights to lose.

Most credit card companies' necessary information for the consumer to complain is located somewhere in the fine print on the back of the bill. Do not send the letter disputing the accuracy of the bill to the same address for payment of the bill, unless specifically directed to do so. It is almost never correct to send a letter disputing a credit card error to the same address to which credit card statements are mailed.

A telephone call or an email to dispute the bill is not effective under the law. It does not protect your legal rights. The complaint letter must be sent in writing via the United States Postal Service or a service such as FedEx in order to protect your rights under the law. The credit card company usually requires that you dispute the item in writing within sixty days. Each company has different rules. It is up to you to track down the information.

The *Fair Credit Billing Act* is a federal law that confers important rights on consumers with a credit card billing problem. You must dispute the charge in writing within sixty days of receipt of the bill. The letter notifying the credit card company of the disputed charge must be received within the sixty-day period by the credit card company at their billing inquiries address. Be very careful to mail your letter so it is processed within the sixty-day period. Many credit card companies take as many as ten days to process payments and correspondence from customers. Mail the letter to the correct address—not the payment address, unless the credit card company directs you to do so.

The credit card company has thirty days to acknowledge your complaint after the letter has been received, and it has two billing cycles to resolve the complaint. During this time you cannot be billed for the charge or any interest for this item. You must, of course, pay for items not in dispute.

The creditor cannot report you as delinquent to a credit bureau during this time. If you exercise your right to question a charge, it cannot be used as a reason to deny you credit. Retaliation for contesting a bill is prohibited under the law. The creditor cannot make any attempt to collect the disputed amount during the investigation period.

The Federal Trade Commission (FTC) has a website for further information at **www.ftc.gov/bcp/conline/pubs/credit/fcb.htm**.

Unauthorized Charges

You must dispute the accuracy of a charge on your credit card bill in writing. Be very careful to follow the requirement of your card. The fine print on the back of the bill should contain this information. Note that the address you send payments to is often different from the address to which you send complaints and disputes.

Credit cards can be very helpful in situations when an unauthorized charge has been made to your card. If a retail company refuses to issue a credit, the credit card company can investigate. You can dispute the bill while the company investigates. During this time, you do not have to pay the disputed amount.

Damaged Merchandise

Keep records of purchases made on your credit card and delivery documents for those items. If merchandise is received damaged and you refuse it upon delivery, write "refused delivery because of damaged merchandise" across the front of the delivery documents. Contact the company to discuss the damaged merchandise. Most companies are reputable and want the customer to be satisfied. If you cannot work something out with the company, you can dispute the charge on your credit card.

Payment Processing

Credit card companies have occasionally taken longer than necessary to process payments. This increases the late fees due from the consumers. If you believe a company is purposely processing your payments late, contact them immediately. Keep track of the amount of time it takes for you to send in a payment and for them to process it.

Many credit card companies sneak language into the fine print of the terms of the credit card agreements, stating that payments must be received and processed by noon or earlier on the due date. If the payment is not posted to your account by the deadline, you will be charged a hefty late fee. The late fee may be charged even though your payment was received by the credit card company on time. Read the fine print, and do not throw away the inserts that come with your bills along with coupons and solicitations for items you do not need or want. If you receive online bills, you must save this information and read it carefully. Do not delete it, because this is now a part of your contract with the credit card company.

Lost or Stolen Cards

The minute you know that your card is lost or stolen, or that someone has unauthorized use of the card, call your credit card company to report the situation. You may be responsible for the unauthorized charges if you fail to report the problem promptly.

Divorce and Credit

Divorce causes many common credit problems. The credit card company does not care if you are divorced, as long as you are each authorized to use the card. The credit card company does not care what your divorce judgment says about who is responsible for the card, who cannot use the credit card, or other domestic issues. It is up to the person whose name is on the card to cancel any additional users of the card.

Your divorce lawyer should have included a paragraph in your divorce judgment or final decree that prohibits each spouse from using the other's credit cards after the divorce. You should have closed all joint accounts and all accounts on which your ex-spouse is an authorized signer. You fail to take these steps at your peril.

DEBIT CARDS

Debit cards look just like credit cards, but your rights are very different if your card is lost or stolen. Credit card holders cannot be held responsible for more than $50 in losses once the card is reported as lost or stolen to the credit card issuer. Debit card holders can lose their entire bank balances to a thief, unless the card is reported lost or stolen with two days.

Despite being advised not to write down the PIN numbers where they can be found easily, most people continue to do this. Even if a dishonest family member finds your PIN, it is still an unauthorized use of the card—but you could lose all of your money. If the bank believes that someone you know used your personal identification number (PIN) to access your account, even without your permission, you can lose the entire sum. The bank can try to hold you responsible for the loss. Banks sometimes try to turn the tables on the customer and accuse the customer of assisting in the theft of the card.

If your debit card has been used without your knowledge or permission, fight back. If your complaint letter does not get results, complain to the appropriate consumer or government agency. The *Office of the Comptroller of the Currency* (OCC) governs national banks. If you are the customer of a national bank, this is the place to take your complaint to the next level.

OCC Customer Assistance Group
Customer Assistance Group
1301 McKinney Street
Suite 3450
Houston, TX 77010
800-613-6743
Fax: 713-336-4301
www.occ.treas.gov/customer.htm

You can file a complaint with the OCC Customer Assistance Group online at **www.occ.treas.gov/consumercomplaintform.pdf**. You can also file a complaint by downloading the form at this website and mailing it to the address provided. If you need more help, call their toll-free number.

COLLECTING A DEBT

A creditor is permitted to collect its own debts; however, this does not give it license to use abusive collection techniques. Behaviors such as calling the debtor repeatedly at all hours of the day and night, threatening the debtor with jail, and impersonating a lawyer are prohibited by the Fair Debt Collection Practices Act.

The *Fair Debt Collection Practices Act* is a federal law that establishes the guidelines that those trying to collect a debt must follow in their dealings and contact with a debtor. Under the Act, debt collectors must identify themselves as such when they call, and may not contact you before 8 a.m. and after 9 p.m. Also, collectors cannot call you at work, if you are not permitted to accept personal calls there. They may not call you repeatedly, or harass, oppress, or abuse you. They may not threaten or use violence to collect a debt. You can instruct a debt collector to not call you again, and the collector must abide by your request. However, the collector can still contact you by mail regarding the status of your account.

The Federal Trade Commission enforces this law. Contact the FTC at:

Federal Trade Commission
600 Pennsylvania Avenue, NW
Washington, DC 20580
877-FTC-HELP (382-4357)
www.ftc.gov/bcp/conline/edcams/credit

State and local laws may also regulate debt collectors and their practices. States usually license debt collection agencies, but many agencies do not bother to register. Those that do not register cannot legally conduct business in the state. Be sure to report these unlicensed agencies.

CREDIT REPORTS

You have a right to receive a free credit report if you are turned down for credit or turned down for a job based on this information. You should receive a letter informing you of the reason for your denial if it is based on information from a particular credit-reporting firm. You should also receive information on how to contact the firm for a free report. Send for the report, as many credit reports have errors. You have a right to correct your credit file, and you should exercise this right.

You can dispute inaccurate information in your credit reports without paying someone to do it for you. The key is that *incorrect* information can be disputed. If the facts in your file are correct, only the passage of time will eliminate this information. Negative credit information stays in your file for seven years, and bankruptcy stays in your file for ten years.

Many websites are available to help consumers. Try your state government resources. The FTC has information for those who want to repair their credit online at **www.ftc.gov/bcp/conline/pubs/credit/repair.htm**.

If you have been denied credit in the past sixty days, you are entitled to a free copy of your credit report. The letter denying you credit should advise you of the name of the credit reporting agency, its address, and its telephone numbers. If there is a mistake on your credit file, ask the credit reporting agency to send you a form for correction. There may be a website that has a downloadable or online correction form. Once you have disputed the information in your file, the company has to delete it if the information cannot be verified.

Federal law requires the nation's three largest credit bureaus to provide you with a free copy of your credit report once every twelve months, even if you have not been turned down for credit. You can order your free credit report online at **annualcreditreport.com**, by calling 877-322-8228, or by completing the *Annual Credit Report Request Form* and mailing it to:

Annual Credit Report Request Service
P.O. Box 105283
Atlanta, GA 30348

You must give your name, address, Social Security number, and date of birth. You will also be asked for a piece of information to verify your identity. Do not use the amount of your monthly mortgage payment, because that amount may be available in a public record.

The FTC has a website with more information on free credit reports at **www.ftc.gov/bcp/conline/edcams/credit/ycr_free_reports.htm**. You will also find information about building better credit, including the rules that govern companies offering services to repair your credit, on this website.

INSURANCE BILLS

Open all bills promptly. Ask for an itemized copy of the bill, especially for a hospital visit. If you find errors, dispute the bill as soon as possible. Contact your insurance company to assist you in resolving the problem. The insurance companies have *provider relations departments.* If there are too many complaints from people the company insures about a particular hospital or doctor, then the company can (and often does) drop them from the managed care provider lists. It only takes a telephone call from the insurance company to one of their contacts to resolve the problem.

Billing errors commonly stem from the health care provider not billing the insurance company correctly. This results in a lower rate of reimbursement. Occasionally, hospitals fail to apply the managed care negotiated discount to the bill. Problems such as these should be addressed immediately.

NOTE: *See if your insurance plan requires dispute letters to be sent by certified mail.*

INVESTMENTS

The federal *Securities and Exchange Commission* (SEC) regulates publicly traded stocks, mutual funds, and other securities. The SEC protects investors and maintains the integrity of the market. It regulates stockbrokers and other professionals in the field.

The SEC is headquartered in Washington, D.C., with regional offices across the country. Consult its website at **www.sec.gov** to learn the region to which your state is assigned, and for information about the regional offices. Complaint forms may be downloaded from the website, but you may also send a letter explaining your problem. Complaints should be directed to the SEC Complaint Center online or to the following address.

SEC Complaint Center
100 F Street, NE
Washington, DC 20546
800-SEC-0330
www.sec.gov/complaint.shtml

Many investors who are dissatisfied with their returns have filed *arbitration demands*. You should have a lawyer for this process. Many lawyers do not charge a fee unless a recovery is made for you. Look on the Internet or in your telephone book for names of securities lawyers. Many major newspapers and financial dailies carry advertisements offering lawyers' services in this area. Your local bar association and law schools may also have a referral for you.

Investment advisors and stock brokers have a duty to recommend suitable stocks. An elderly, retired person usually needs conservative investments. Clients may state they want high-tech speculative stocks. They may be unhappy when the high-tech stocks lose most of their value, but that is the risk they took. The broker has not violated the law for placing a speculative stock order if that is what the client wants and the client has been informed that it is a risky stock.

MEMBERS OF THE MILITARY

The *Soldiers' and Sailors' Civil Relief Act of 1940* was enacted to provide protection for members of the military from financial problems while on active duty. (This protection also extends to reservists called to active duty.) It was amended in 2003 and is now called the *Servicemembers' Civil Relief Act* (SCRA), but you may still hear it refered to as the Soldiers' and Sailors' Civil Relief Act. The amended Act updates the protections from the old act and extends some of the protection offered. The protection includes:

- reduced interest rate on mortgage payments;

- reduced interest rate on credit card debt;

- protection from eviction if rent is $1,200 or less; and,

- delay of all civil court actions, including bankruptcy, foreclosure, or divorce proceedings.

The procedure for reducing your interest rate is discussed below. If you find that you are involved in either an eviction or civil action, you can notify the court in which the matter was filed of your active status. However, to be sure that the proceedings do not continue without your involvement, contact an attorney.

Those on active duty are entitled to pay no more than 6% interest on their debt. The military member must notify the mortgage company or credit card company of the request to trigger the 6% or less rate. Send a copy of the order requiring you to report to active duty via certified mail. If the military member is out of the country or otherwise unable to write, a spouse, family member, or person with the power of attorney should contact the creditor. A reservist called to active duty should include information about the difference between his or her normal salary and the active duty salary.

The creditor has the right to challenge the 6% interest rate. However, the burden of proof is on the mortgage company or the credit card company to prove in court that the military person is financially unaffected by the call to active duty. Most judges will require the creditor to lower the interest rate to 6%.

This reduction of interest rate is good for all debts incurred prior to military service if the bill is still outstanding. The creditor must reduce the rate to 6% upon receipt of the letter from the military debtor or go to court to prove that the debtor is financially unaffected by the call to active duty. Most creditors will not want to risk a public relations fiasco by challenging a military member's federally guaranteed rights.

The *American Forces Information Service* has a website with detailed information at **www.defenselink.mil/specials/relief_act_revision**.

Some states now prohibit utility companies from turning off service when the account is not paid and a member of the household is on active military duty. Check your state laws to learn if you have additional protections from credit problems.

TAKING ACTION—STEP-BY-STEP

1. Keep all your records. Review your statements as they arrive. Monitor your accounts online. There are very definite time limits for reporting forgery or theft to your bank accounts and credit cards.

2. Contact your bank or brokerage. Ask to speak with your personal banker or the branch manager. If there has been theft in your account, you must call the special telephone number your bank provides. Document the date and time of your call so that you can prove later that you notified the bank of the problem. If the bank employee is not responsive, then ask to speak with a supervisor.

    Note: *If you still cannot get help, contact the general counsel's office and speak to a lawyer.*

3. Always keep copies of your letters. Send important correspondence by certified mail. Keep records of telephone calls and with whom you spoke.

    Note: *Consumer lawyers may represent you in a lawsuit for no charge (unless you win) when you sue a bank or credit card company for various violations.*

4. Contact the appropriate government agency. The Federal Trade Commission monitors credit cards. Bank regulators on the state and federal level may also be of assistance.

5. In cases of credit card theft or identity theft, contact the Federal Trade Commission and your local prosecutor. The state attorney general may have an identity theft unit, too. You should also contact your banks and credit card companies. The Social Security Administration should be notified that someone may be using your number.

Letter 5.1:
Credit Card Company—
Dispute Charge

Amanda Beck
915 West Huron Street
Chicago, IL 60612
773-605-2136

May 1, 2007

Metropolitan Bank Visa Card
P.O. Box 8853
Smalltown, SD 82345

Re: Account #909338675

Dear Sir or Madam:

Please be advised that I dispute the accuracy of an item on the May statement, received today. There is a charge for $856 for a sofa from Elegant Furniture in Chicago. The sofa arrived ripped in many places. I refused delivery. A copy of the delivery order with "refused because of damage" written across is enclosed. There should be a credit issued for this item by Elegant Furniture.

My account should reflect this fact.

Very truly yours,

Amanda Beck

Letter 5.2:
Credit Card Company—Dispute Charge;
Second Letter

Amanda Beck
915 West Huron Street
Chicago, IL 60612
773-605-2136

June 1, 2007

Metropolitan Bank Visa Card
P.O. Box 8853
Smalltown, SD 82345

Re: Account #909338675

Dear Sir or Madam:

On May 1, 2007, I sent you a letter disputing the accuracy of a charge for $856 to my account. This was for a sofa I ordered that arrived damaged. I refused delivery. Elegant Furniture of Chicago should have credited my account for this sum in April.

Please exert some pressure on Elegant Furniture to issue this credit. I also continue to dispute the accuracy of this bill. I am enclosing a copy of my previous letter and another copy of the delivery order.

Very truly yours,

Amanda Beck

Letter 5.3:
Credit Card Company— Error on Statement

Carol Franklin
4433 Main Street
Anywhere, DE 02345
555-222-0000

April 2, 2007

Bank of Giant Profits
Visa Card
P.O. Box 1233
Nowhere, SD 78943

Re: Error in Billing Account #3487912

Dear Sir or Madam:

Please be advised that there is an error on my April statement. You have listed a charge to my account from the Corner Table Restaurant in Wilmington, Delaware, for $805. This is a mistake. I am enclosing a copy of my original charge slip for $8.50. Please correct this error.

Thank you,

Carol Franklin

Letter 5.4:
Credit Card Company—
Late Charge Assessed

Amanda Beck
915 West Huron Street
Chicago, IL 60612
773-605-2136

July 1, 2007

Metropolitan Bank Visa Card
P.O. Box 8853
Smalltown, SD 82345

Re: Account #909338675

Dear Sir or Madam:

Please be advised that my July statement contains a late payment fee of $35. You assessed this charge because you claim to have not received my payment until five days after the due date. The payment was mailed ten days before the due date, and the check was presented for payment at my bank one day after the due date. How could you process the check and have it at my bank one day after the due date, and claim the payment was five days late?

I suspect that, as has been reported in the financial news, you are deliberately failing to process payments in a timely manner. When the customer's check sits on someone's desk for days you can make a handsome profit by charging an undeserved late fee.

I expect that this late fee will be removed and that you will not charge me another fee again.

Very truly yours,

Amanda Beck

Letter 5.5:
Credit Card Company—
Unauthorized Use After a Divorce

Careful Consumer
48 Frugal Street
Parsimony, PA 25000
555-888-2222

June 1, 2007

USA Credit Card Company
P.O. Box 7540
Anywhere, ND 90909

Re: Unauthorized Charge

Dear Sir or Madam:

I am writing to inform you of unauthorized activity on my account. All of the charges on May 20 in New Orleans, LA, are not mine. My ex-husband, John, made them on a canceled card.

On May 1, 2007, I notified you by telephone and by certified letter that I was canceling charge privileges for my husband, John, effective immediately. We are now divorced. I am not responsible for the charges for the Big Easy Hotel and Bar.

Enclosed please find a copy of the signed, certified receipt for my letter of May 1 and a current telephone and address for my ex-husband.

Please correct the statement.

Very truly yours,

Careful Consumer

Letter 5.6:
Bank—
Unauthorized Transaction on Debit Card

Jane Lostbucks
313 Naylor Street
New Orleans, LA 70113
777-111-0000

March 5, 2007

Louisiana National Bank
1 Bourbon Street
New Orleans, LA 70111

Re: Debit Card #1234

Dear Sir or Madam:

Please be advised that my debit card with a MasterCard logo was used for unauthorized transactions on December 12 and 13, 2006. Someone was able to access my account to purchase stereo equipment at Joe's Stereo City online on these dates in the amounts of $1,200 and $500, respectively. The store records show that the merchandise was shipped to an address unknown to me. I did not learn of this until my statement arrived yesterday.

I have provided this information to your fraud unit in a telephone conversation yesterday with Mr. Smith.

No one else has access to my card. Please credit my account with $1,700 to reimburse me for these fraudulent charges.

Very truly yours,

Jane Lostbucks

Letter 5.7:
Bank—Debit Card Used
to Empty Checking Account

George Williamson
400 North Avenue
Atlanta, GA 70113
555-555-1234

March 7, 2007

Georgia National Bank
1 Peach Street
Atlanta, GA 70111

Re: Debit Card #1234

Dear Sir or Madam:

I am writing to advise you that an unauthorized transaction on my debit card emptied my checking account of $2,200 on March 3, 2007. No one has access to my PIN number or card except me.

Please investigate and restore my $2,200 at once. I learned of this theft when I checked my balance online yesterday. This letter is a follow-up to the telephone call I made to your security office yesterday.

Very truly yours,

George Williamson

Letter 5.8:
Dispute with Bank—
Unauthorized Use of Debit Card

George Williamson
400 North Avenue
Atlanta, GA 70113
555-555-1234

March 20, 2007

Georgia National Bank
1 Peach Street
Atlanta, GA 70111

Re: Debit Card #1234

Dear Sir or Madam:

Once again I am writing to insist that you return $2,200 for an unauthorized debit deducted from my account on March 3, 2007. You have declined to restore this sum to my account because I allegedly gave the PIN number or card to someone known to me. This is patently false.

At no time have I shared my PIN number or a card with anyone. It is more likely that a waiter at a restaurant copied my number, or a clerk at a store where I used my debit card memorized my PIN as I punched it in. This is my last demand for restoration of the account. The next step is for me to file a formal complaint with the Office of the Comptroller of the Currency.

I want to resolve this amicably, but will not hesitate to take further action if necessary.

Very truly yours,

George Williamson

Letter 5.9:
Dispute with Collection Agency—
Alleged Debt

Constance Coed
19 Campus Drive
Augusta, ME 13759
333-676-7777

March 16, 2007

Ruthless Collection Agency
900 Mean Street
Elmira, NY 32000

Re: Dispute of Alleged Debt
Your File #313000

Dear Sir or Madam:

I am writing to dispute the accuracy of a debt I allegedly owe to University Credit Card Company for $502.28. This is incorrect. Please investigate this error and correct your records.

Please do not contact me again in an attempt to collect this debt.

Very truly yours,

Constance Coed
Via certified mail

Letter 5.10:
Collection Agency—
Disputing Alleged Debt; Second Letter

Constance Coed
19 Campus Drive
Augusta, ME 13759
333-676-7777

March 29, 2007

Ruthless Collection Agency
900 Mean Street
Elmira, NY 32000

Re: Dispute of Alleged Debt
Your File #313000

Dear Sir or Madam:

This is the second time in a few weeks I have been required to write to you to dispute the accuracy of an alleged debt. On March 16, I notified you by certified mail that I disputed the alleged debt and that I did not want to be contacted again by you to collect this contested debt. A copy of the March 16 letter is enclosed.

On March 28, I received another collection letter from you. Once again, I am stating that I dispute the accuracy of this alleged debt and that I do not want to be contacted again by you in any manner in an attempt to collect this sum.

You have violated the Fair Debt Collection Practices Act by persisting in your efforts to collect this debt. I shall take any further violations very seriously, including pursuing my legal remedies.

Very truly yours,

Constance Coed
Via certified mail

Letter 5.11:
Credit Agency–
Negative Credit Report

Alan Trainspotter
25 Alumni Street
Iowa City, IA 34090
555-555-1212

March 19, 2007

Big Credit Agency
P.O. Box 88
Arlington, TX 50899

Re: Errors in File

Dear Sir or Madam:

I was recently turned down for a car loan. The letter denying my loan stated that your agency has negative credit information about me. Please send me my free copy of this report. My Social Security number is 000-00-0000. A copy of the letter is enclosed.

Thank you,

Alan Trainspotter

Letter 5.12:
Credit Agency—
Errors in Credit Report

Alan Trainspotter
25 Alumni Street
Iowa City, IA 34090
555-555-1212

March 30, 2007

Big Credit Agency
P.O. Box 88
Arlington, TX 50899

Re: Errors in File

Dear Sir or Madam:

I have reviewed the copy of my credit report from your agency. Please note that this information does not appear to be my account. This information belongs to another gentleman with the same last name, but a different spelling of the first name, "Allen," a different Social Security number, and a different birthday.

Please correct these errors immediately.

Very truly yours,

Alan Trainspotter

Letter 5.13:
Insurance Billing Error

Paul Patient
3389 West Maple Drive
Tucson, AZ 86432
444-890-9999

May 8, 2007

Patient Accounts Manager
Local Hospital
200 Gold Street
Hot Town, AZ 86433

Re: Billing Error/Account #30943

Dear Sir or Madam:

I received your bill for my hospital stay of March 11–13. It was not itemized. Please send me a detailed statement, including each and every charge made to me for this stay. Until I see the detailed bill, I cannot be certain, but I believe that you have charged me the wrong rate.

My managed care plan has negotiated substantial discounts with your institution. You have apparently charged me the full rate, instead of the discounted amount. I have compared your bill with that paid by my insurance company.

Please correct your bill and send me a detailed statement.

Very truly yours,

Paul Patient

Letter 5.14:
Insurance Billing Error; Second Letter

Paul Patient
3389 West Maple Drive
Tucson, AZ 86432
444-890-9999

June 3, 2007

Patient Accounts Manager
Local Hospital
200 Gold Street
Hot Town, AZ 86433

Re: Billing Error #30943

Dear Sir or Madam:

Once again I am writing to you about a billing error for my hospital stay in March. I have disputed this bill previously in my correspondence to you dated May 8. A copy of this letter is enclosed.

To date you have not provided a detailed bill. Once again, I dispute the accuracy of your charges. Based on the insurance payments and explanation of benefits provided to me by my managed care insurance company, I believe that you have charged me the full rate. I should have been charged the discounted rate negotiated by my insurance company.

Please correct this error. I am still waiting for an itemized bill.

Very truly yours,

Paul Patient

Letter 5.15:
Liquidation of Brokerage Account

Jane Investor
4 Easy Street
Palm Springs, CA 00000
123-123-4567

August 11, 2007

Dewey Fleeceum and Howe
Investment Company
18 Main Street
New York, NY 11111

Re: My Brokerage Account

Dear Sirs:

I am writing to advise you that I am closing my account with you immediately. Please liquidate my holdings and send the check to my new broker, Mr. Honest Broker.

You know that I am a retired widow on a small Social Security and pension income. Still, you managed to invest in speculative funds that caused a loss in my IRA account in the past six months. It went from $180,000 to $90,000, or a loss of 50% of the value.

You placed me in inappropriate investments for someone my age and in my financial situation.

Very truly yours,

Jane Investor

Letter 5.16:
Liquidation of Brokerage Account;
Follow-Up to Securities Exchange

Jane Investor
4 Easy Street
Palm Springs, CA 00000
123-123-4567

September 15, 2007

Securities and Exchange Commission
Headquarters
450 Fifth Street, NW
Washington, DC 20549

Re: Broker Complaint

Dear Sir or Madam:

I am writing to complain about the conduct of my broker, Dewey Fleeceum and Howe. On August 11, 2007, I sent the firm a letter requesting that my IRA account be closed and the funds sent to my new broker immediately. To date I have not received any response.

The Dewey firm invested inappropriately for me, causing a loss of 50% of the value of my account in six months. I have enclosed a complaint form that I downloaded from your Internet site.

Anything you can do to help me to get the balance of my funds from Dewey would be greatly appreciated. Copies of the correspondence are enclosed.

Very truly yours,

Jane Investor

Letter 5.17:
Securities Exchange Commission—
Reporting Brokerage Violations

John Investor
22 North Avenue
Providence, RI 12345
101-333-8644

April 18, 2007

Securities and Exchange Commission
Headquarters
450 Fifth Street, NW
Washington, DC 20549

Re: Brokerage Violation

Dear Sir or Madam:

I am writing to you to complain about self-dealing by my brokerage house and stockbroker, Cheatum and Scarum.

On July 1, 2006, I opened a brokerage account at Cheatum and Scarum. I deposited $350,000, which represented my retirement savings. I explained to the broker when I opened the account that I needed to carefully and conservatively manage this money. I also explained this in writing at the time I opened the account.

Almost from the moment I opened the account, I received calls from my broker, Jeffrey Lying, touting one stock or another. He claimed that in-house research recommended these "hot" stocks. Mr. Lying invited me to lunch on many occasions and after several drinks, I agreed to invest in his recommended stocks. These stocks were losers. I lost over half the value of my investment in a short period of time. Please investigate.

Very truly yours,

John Investor

Letter 5.18:
Credit Card Company—Reduction in
Interest Rate due to Military Service

Mary Jones
230 Cresthill Circle
Great Lakes, IL 61300
847-555-5050

June 30, 2007

Avarice Credit Card Company
P.O. Box 1185
Sioux City, IA 24550

Re: Military Relief Account #995577

Dear Sir or Madam:

Please be advised that I am a member of the U.S. Navy, and have been on active duty since March 1 of this year. The interest rate on my credit card account is 20% APR. While serving my country on active duty, I am requesting that you charge the 6% per year interest rate to which I am entitled by the Servicemembers' Civil Relief Act.

My bill should be adjusted to reflect the 6% interest rate retroactively to March 1. A copy of the order calling me to active duty is enclosed.

Thank you,

Mary Jones

6
Identity Theft and Computer-Based Fraud

The crime of identity theft is more prevalent today than it was several years ago. There is no doubt that these dishonest schemes will multiply in the next few years. Thieves are more intent than ever on separating you from your money. Criminals can steal more money with a pen or a computer than they can with a gun. A new term—*crimeware*—has been coined to describe the software used to cheat you.

It is a federal crime under the *Identity Theft and Assumption Deterrence Act* when someone "knowingly transfers or uses, without lawful authority, a means of identification of another person with the intent to commit, or to aid or abet, any unlawful activity that constitutes a violation of federal law, or that constitutes a felony under any applicable state or local law."

Your identity and financial information can be stolen in numerous ways, including:

- *phishing*—high-tech scam that uses spam to deceive consumers into disclosing their sensitive personal information;

- *spyware*—attaches *cookies* to your computer to track your information;

- *skimming*—collecting your information by secretly attaching a data-saving device to an automatic teller machine (ATM) or credit/debit card processing device;

- *pretexting*—tricking you into providing the information under false pretenses; and,

- fraudulent Internet auctions.

To protect your computer from identity thieves, you should install a good antivirus and firewall program. Do not download a free program, because this may contain a virus. It is better to buy the software from a legitimate vendor. The cost is low, especially when you consider the damage an infected computer or your stolen identity can cause.

IDENTITY THEFT

Your personal information—including bank accounts, credit cards, debit cards, Social Security number, and insurance cards—can be stolen the old-fashioned way, such as stealing your purse or wallet, or stolen online. No matter the manner of the theft of this crucial data, you must take certain steps immediately once you have discovered the theft.

The Federal Trade Commission (FTC), the United States government agency that advocates for consumers, maintains an informative website to assist victims of identity theft at **www.onguardonline.gov/idtheft.html**. *Onguard* is a new joint venture between the FTC and the Canadian government to protect citizens from identity theft. The site offers valuable information for consumers to protect their information. If you are a victim of identity theft, the site has instructions for you to follow.

The FTC also has a Web page devoted to identity theft at **www.consumer.gov/idtheft**.

Each state's attorney general has a website that provides help for victims of identity theft. Please see Appendix A for a complete list of each state's attorney general.

Many states are considering legislation to require financial institutions, hospitals, insurance companies, and other entities to report the theft of information to customers. California is the first state to have strict disclosure laws. Illinois passed a law in 2005 that requires companies to report the theft of sensitive financial information to customers and to increase the criminal penalties for identification theft.

There are numerous ways to part you from your hard-earned funds. Crooks are using crimeware to capture your money in new ways every day. Never give your financial information to anyone who asks for it first.

PHISHING

Phishing is defined as a computer-based theft of personal information using lillicit copies of legitimate computer sites and email addresses to fool the consumer into divulging sensitive financial information, such as credit card numbers, passwords, PIN information, and Social Security numbers.

Thieves use the Internet to troll for victims. You may be tricked into providing information to what you think is a legitimate source. A favorite scam is for a thief to create a copy of a legitimate website, such as your bank's site. You may receive an email from what you believe is your bank. The email asks you to confirm your account number, Social Security number, or personal identification number (PIN).

Never respond to this email. Banks do not contact customers by email, except for routine advertising messages. If you receive a suspicious message from what looks like your bank, print it out and call the bank. *Do not* click on a link. The links look like they go to a legitimate source, but are directed to the thief's computer instead. *Do not* click on such a pop-up ad for the same reason.

Along with providing a copy of the *phishing* email to your bank, you should report the activity to **reportphishing@antiphishing.org**. The *Anti-Phishing Working Group* (APWG) is an association of private and law enforcement groups that uses these reports to track down computer criminals. You can visit their website at **www.antiphishing.org**.

The *Internal Revenue Service* (IRS) has issued a consumer alert notifying taxpayers that criminals are sending out fake email notices supposedly contacting taxpayers to verify financial information or to inform them of their refund status. The IRS never contacts taxpayers by email for the first time. You may receive an email about the status of your return if you have filed electronically or asked to be contacted. However, the IRS will never ask for sensitive financial information in an email. The crooks are getting sneakier, so be aware of all cyberspace communications soliciting your financial details. If you are in doubt, call the agency directly or go to the website. Never click on the link in a suspect email, because it will probably lead you directly to the criminal's computer.

PRETEXTING

Pretexting is the process of obtaining your personal information under false pretenses. This may be done over the Internet, by a telephone caller conducting a "survey," by placing a phony sweepstakes box at a shopping center inviting you to fill out an entry card, or by sending you a letter informing you that you have won a contest, but you must provide money or personal information in order to collect. The range of the scams is limited only by the criminal's creativity.

The *Gramm-Leach Bliley Act* is a federal law that makes it illegal to use false statements or forged documents, or to ask a third party to obtain customer information from a financial institution or from the customer of a financial institution.

STOLEN PURSES, BRIEFCASES, AND LUGGAGE

You may have your pocket picked or your purse stolen in a busy store or restaurant. Women may leave their purses slung over a chair at a restaurant. A skilled thief can remove the wallet without your knowledge, or the entire purse may be stolen while you dine.

If you travel, you must be alert going through security. You are asked to leave your purse or wallet in a tray while it is whisked through a security check and disgorged at the end of a conveyor belt. It is out of your sight for a minute or more, so you must check when it comes out at the end of the conveyor belt.

You should not pack anything valuable in your checked luggage. Security guards have been caught stealing from the checked baggage at the airport. There have been several reports of security guards stealing from luggage over the past few years. The *Transportation Security Administration* (TSA), the federal agency responsible for airport security, has quietly reimbursed passengers for stolen items. Consult the TSA website at **www.tsaclaims.org** for information on downloading a claim form and how to file a claim.

You may think it is safe to leave your laptop or briefcase unattended for a moment or two. Never leave these items unguarded at a restaurant, coffee house, library, airport, or other public place.

PATIENTS VICTIMIZED

If your purse, wallet, or briefcase has been stolen, you must assume that your identification, credit cards, checking information, and debit cards are going to be used by a thief. Some thieves steal these items looking for the identification more than the cash they may contain. There is a ready market for stolen identification information, including stolen Social Security numbers.

Today there are more subtle ways to sneak into your private life. Your Social Security number may be stolen at a doctor's office or hospital when you provide your number to a clerk. Many insurance companies have changed the identification numbers on the insurance cards provided to policyholders to avoid displaying Social Security numbers on the cards. Despite this helpful step, many hospitals and medical offices persist in recording your Social Security number in many places throughout their system. Dishonest employees can steal this information and sell it to thieves. The University of Chicago Hospitals reported the theft of patient information in February of 2005. The FBI reported that an unscrupulous employee was under suspicion for stealing the personal information of eighty-five patients. The hospital offered to run credit reports for other patients who may have been victimized.

In October of 2005, the Wilcox Memorial Hospital in Kauai, Hawaii reported that a missing backup computer drive containing confidential financial and personal information of 130,000 former and current patients was missing from its hospital. This included the Social Security numbers, names, and home addresses of these patients.

If you have been a patient at a large, urban hospital recently, either as an outpatient or inpatient, you have probably been asked for a photo ID as well as your insurance card. You may also be asked some other personal information that only you would know when you register at an outpatient clinic. This is because thieves have started to sell insurance cards to the uninsured, and even use the insurance cards themselves.

TAKING ACTION—STEP-BY-STEP

1. If you believe your personal information has been compromised or stolen, cancel all credit cards and notify your banks, credit unions, and health and property insurers.

2. Contact the Federal Trade Commission (FTC) to report identity theft at **www.consumer.gov/idtheft**. You may also call the FTC's Identity Theft Hotline, toll-free at 877-ID-THEFT (438-4338) or 866-653-4261 (TTY). File a complaint by writing to:

Identity Theft Clearinghouse
Federal Trade Commission
600 Pennsylvania Avenue, NW
Washington, DC 20580

3. Place a fraud alert on all your credit accounts by contacting the three major national credit reporting agencies.

Equifax
P.O. Box 740241
Atlanta, GA 30374
800-685-1111
www.equifax.com

Experian
P.O. Box 9532
Allen, TX 75013
888-EXPERIAN (397-3742)
www.experian.com

TransUnion
P.O. Box 2000
Chester, PA 19022
800-888-4213
www.transunion.com

You are entitled to receive a free credit report after reporting the identity theft to the FTC. Review the report carefully to see if you have remembered all the accounts you have and to see if the thieves are applying for credit in your name.

4. File a police report with your local police. In big cities, police may try to discourage you from reporting because it means more paperwork for them. In response to this problem, many cities and states are considering legislation to require the police to take these reports. Check with your local government officials to determine if there is a law requiring the police to take these reports.

5. Report your stolen driver's license to the state agency from which you obtained your license. Place a fraud alert on the license if available. Obtain a new license and do not put your Social Security number on the front.

Letter 6.1:
Reporting Theft
to Credit Card Company

Laura Petrie
12 Canasta Lane
New Rochelle, NY 21030
123-456-7890

July 15, 2007

Unconscionable Credit Card Company
17 Road to Perdition
Devil's Lake, NM 66666

Re: Stolen Card

Dear Sir or Madam:

This letter will confirm my telephone call to your fraud hotline on July 14, 2007, to report the theft of my Platinum Card account #4805. Please confirm that you have placed a fraud alert on my account for this, and my new account.

Please send my new card by express mail.

Very truly yours,

Laura Petrie

Letter 6.2:
Asking Police Department
to File Theft Report

Robert Hartley
5400 North Sheridan Road
Chicago, IL 60626
111-333-5544

April 1, 2007

Commander
Chicago Police Department Headquarters
330 West Loop
Chicago, IL 60600

Re: Identity Theft Report

Dear Commander:

My financial information was stolen when computer information was stolen from the bank holding my retirement funds. I believe the information was on a laptop loaded with retirement account information for thousands of customers, which was stolen from a bank employee's car. I tried to file a police report at the Rogers Park station, but was told by the desk sergeant that he could not take a report.

Please direct me to an officer who will take an identity theft report. I need it in order to establish that there was a theft. The credit card companies and my bank also want copies of this report.

Very truly yours,

Robert Hartley

Letter 6.3:
Reporting Identity Theft
to Federal Trade Commission

Barbie Doll
18 Dream House Street
Toyland, CA 92888
222-444-6666

July 5, 2007

Identity Theft Clearinghouse
Federal Trade Commission
600 Pennsylvania Avenue, NW
Washington, DC 20580

Re: Complaint

To whom it may concern:

Please be advised that I am filing my complaint about the theft of my identification. My purse was stolen from the table of our restaurant while I was having dinner with my boyfriend, Ken.

Enclosed is a list of my stolen credit cards, bank accounts, etc., and a copy of your complaint form, which I downloaded from your website.

Sincerely,

Barbie Doll

Letter 6.4:
Bank—Failure to Notify of
Stolen Financial Information

Ebenezer Scrooge
One Creepy Old Mansion Road
Fidelity, PA 21677
555-111-0000

August 12, 2007

Big Bank of New York
One Financial Street
New York, NY 10000

Re: Failure to Notify of Stolen Information

Dear Sir or Madam:

I am a large depositor in your bank. I trusted you with sensitive financial and personal information. Recently I learned from news accounts that a computer containing thousands of customer accounts was stolen from your main office. You should have notified your customers to be on the alert for fraudulent activity in their accounts as a result of this theft.

Today I opened my monthly statement, which arrived in the mail. I saw that many withdrawals had been made from my accounts, but not by me. Please freeze the account immediately. I expect to be reimbursed for my losses. I will transfer my business elsewhere at the earliest opportunity.

Very truly yours,

Ebenezer Scrooge

7
Health

There are many new federal and state laws that have been enacted in response to consumer complaints regarding health care. Federal law requires new privacy measures by health care providers to protect your right to privacy. You need to be informed about these changes.

Keep copies of all medical bills, receipts, and claim forms. Do not send original documents to the insurance company unless required. Retain all statements from the insurance company that show claim activity and payments on your behalf, known as *explanations of benefits*. (Most insurers do not keep records of this activity, so you cannot get a copy at a later date.)

Insurance companies may try to avoid paying for expensive medications and procedures. Do research to support your request for treatment. If your request is denied, you will have to file a written appeal that conforms to your insurance company's procedures. Enlist the aid of your doctor to write a letter explaining the need for the treatment.

There are state insurance regulators with consumer complaint departments, and state attorneys general may also have consumer health complaint divisions. These public servants intercede on your behalf to persuade the insurers to reconsider the denial of coverage. Insurance companies can be fined and have their licenses to do business in the state revoked for denying coverage that should be provided.

HEALTH INSURANCE PORTABILITY AND ACCOUNTABILITY ACT

The *Health Insurance Portability and Accountability Act of 1996* (HIPAA) provides strong privacy protections for patients. Your medical information and records must be kept confidential. The doctor, hospital, or other health provider cannot disclose any information about you without your written permission.

Each health care provider must provide a privacy notice to you by mail or in person at your first visit. Keep a copy of this notice when you receive it. The provider must also designate a *privacy officer* to address any complaints of privacy violations.

The *Department of Health and Human Services* is a federal agency that enforces HIPAA, and the *Office of Civil Rights* (OCR) is a special division that investigates complaints. Anyone can file written complaints with OCR by mail, fax, or email. There are ten regional offices. Check the website **www.hhs.gov/ocr/ privacyhowtofile.htm** to find the region to which you belong. A copy of the federal law may be obtained from the Office for Civil Rights online at **www.hhs.gov/ocr/hipaa**. You can also contact OCR by mail at:

Office for Civil Rights
U.S. Department of Health and Human Services
200 Independence Avenue, SW
Room 509F
Washington, DC 20201
800-368-1019

The complaint must be addressed to the correct regional manager and must:

- be filed in writing, either on paper or electronically;

- name the entity that is the subject of the complaint, and describe the acts or omissions believed to be in violation of the applicable requirements of the Privacy Rule;

- be filed within 180 days of when you knew that the act or omission complained of occurred (OCR may extend the 180-day period if you can show *good cause*); and,

- name an act or omission that occurred on or after April 14, 2003 (on or after April 14, 2004 for small health plans) for OCR to have the authority to investigate.

BILLING ERRORS

Insurance companies and doctors can and do make billing errors. For instance, the doctor's office may not put the correct name of the doctor on the insurance claim form. If the office makes a claim in the name of the practice group instead of the individual physician's name, it may be rejected as out-of-network. Conversely, your insurance company may have your doctor listed under the group name. A claim submitted under the individual doctor's name could be rejected, and your claim could be denied or paid at a much lower rate. This is a very common problem.

Another place for error is in the coding of the illness and treatment by the health care provider. Each illness and procedure has a diagnostic code. The wrong code can mean that your claim is not paid or paid at a fraction of the cost. For such billing problems, ask the billing department to review the bill. If that does not resolve the problem, contact the head of the billing department at your doctor's office or hospital.

Medical providers do not issue itemized bills very often. You should always ask for an itemized bill. Anyone who has been hospitalized recently has not received a detailed bill. Most people never even see the bill. It goes directly to the insurance company, and you are only contacted when the insurance company does not pay the full amount of the bill.

PRESCRIPTION DRUG REFUSAL

When paying for prescriptions, many managed care insurance companies follow a list of authorized drugs called a *formulary*. The company makes a list of frequently prescribed drugs, and then obtains generic or discount prices for the medication. If the drug you need is not listed in the formulary, payment is routinely denied. However, you can challenge this refusal to pay.

Ask your doctor to contact the medical director of the insurance company. This contact information is often unavailable to the policyholder, but it is available if you do some research. Check business publications, public documents, the state insurance department, and with your local reference librarian to find it.

Identify the drug you want to have covered. Describe how it is used to treat your illness. Cite any studies showing the effectiveness of this drug. Using this information and a letter from your doctor, challenge the denial. Just because it is not on the formulary does not mean that you cannot benefit from it. This is especially true if you have a rare illness.

It is imperative that you follow the insurance company requirements for appealing the denial of your coverage. There are usually very strict time requirements for requesting an appeal after being denied coverage. Time may be on your side if you are trying to receive a new drug or treatment. The insurance company may be evaluating covering a drug if medical practice accepts this new treatment. Should the insurance company deny coverage for this drug, ask about covering it under the major medical part of your plan. Sometimes this provides a loophole for coverage.

Do not hesitate to contact your state department of insurance for help. Some state attorneys general also have health care assistance available. A letter or call from a government regulator can be very effective. Save this for last. Try the other avenues of assistance first. However, if time is critical for treatment, do not hesitate to obtain government assistance. (See Appendix C for information on specific state insurance regulators.)

Medicare now provides coverage for many prescription medications. You must sign up for the benefit if you are eligible for Medicare. For more information about this benefit, consult the official government website at **www.medicare.gov**.

DENIAL OF COVERAGE

There are some expensive medications, as well as certain types of surgery and procedures, that are typically not covered by insurance companies. For example, weight reduction surgeries, breast reductions, and fertility treatments are often not covered unless a state law requires it. You must dispute any denial of coverage in writing and in accordance with the rules of your insurance company. There are usually strict time limits in which you can appeal. If you fail to follow the correct procedure, you may waive your right to pursue the denial of payment.

The cooperation of your physician is crucial. You need a letter from your doctor along with the pertinent medical records. If surgery is involved, you need a letter from the surgeon describing the procedure and the need for the surgery.

Today, most insurance companies have websites. Go to your insurance company's website. Many companies have treatment guidelines on the Internet. These are intended for doctors to review treatments. Sometimes clerical personnel will reject a claim for coverage even when the company's medical guidelines cover the surgery. If the company lists your surgery and states the circumstances it will pay for the operation, you should print out this information. Determine whether you meet the guidelines for treatment.

Research your case. Do Internet research through Medline plus (**www.nlm.nih.gov/ medlineplus**) about your illness or condition. Sometimes the insurance company is unaware of new studies or medications. If you and your doctor can show the company the facts substantiating the desired treatment, you may get the company to pay for it.

UNINSURED PATIENT

The *Hill-Burton Act* authorizes federal funding assistance to public and other nonprofit medical facilities, such as acute care general hospitals, special hospitals, nursing homes, public health centers, and rehabilitation facilities. In return for federal funds, the facilities may not deny emergency services to any person residing in the facility's service area on the grounds that the person is unable to pay for those services. No one can be turned away from an emergency room for inability to pay or lack of coverage. The emergency room personnel cannot even ask you about insurance until after you have been evaluated. However, the Act does not require the facility to make nonemergency services available to persons unable to pay for them.

The Act further requires the health care facilities that receive Hill-Burton funds to make services provided by the facility available to persons residing in the facility's service area without discrimination on the basis of race, color, national origin, creed, or any other ground unrelated to the individual's need for the service. The website for this information is operated by the Department of Health and Human Services at **www.os.dhhs.gov/ocr/hburton.html**.

County hospitals often provide care on a sliding scale or for no charge for those without insurance. University hospitals may also be able to offer care at reduced rates. Ask for a social worker to assist you in finding funding or applying for public assistance such as Medicaid.

HOSPITALS

If you are staying in a hospital and have a dirty room, contact the head nurse immediately. He or she can call the housekeeping department to send someone to clean the room. You may also be transferred to another room that is in better condition.

Many larger hospitals have a hospital ombudsman to assist patients in resolving conflicts within the hospital. The ombudsman acts as the patient's advocate with the administration. Ask if there is an ombudsman.

Inform your doctor about any problems at the hospital. Call his or her office and leave a message that you want to be called, even after office hours. The doctor should know what is happening. He or she can call a hospital administrator to fix the problem. Also, most doctors practice at more than one hospital. The doctor should be advised of any problems so he or she can choose to admit patients to another hospital.

The state and trade groups must accredit hospitals. Your state's health department may regulate hospitals. Ask for the name of the agency that supervises hospitals if the state health department does not. An industry group, the *Joint Commission on Accreditation of Healthcare Organizations* (JCAHO), inspects and monitors hospitals. Without accreditation, a hospital will close.

Complaints regarding the cleanliness of, or treatment in, a hospital may be sent to:

Office of Quality Monitoring
JCAHO
One Renaissance Boulevard
Oakbrook Terrace, IL 60181
630-792-5000
www.jointcommission.org

NURSING HOMES

Nursing homes may soon be serving two generations of baby boomer families—elderly parents and their aging children. The quality of care in these homes ranges from superb to abominable. Money alone does not guarantee proper care. Relatives of nursing home patients must be vigilant. Investigate the home before a family member is placed.

State health departments monitor the quality of patient care in nursing homes. All states have an office of aging that is staffed with ombudsmen to help seniors with nursing home and skilled care facility problems. Look for information for your state on the Internet at **www.cms.hhs.gov/contacts**. Another excellent website is the *National Citizen's Coalition for Nursing Home Reform* at **www.nccnhr.org/static_pages/help.cfm**. The organization is located at:

National Citizens Coalition for Nursing Home Reform
1828 L Street, NW
Suite 801
Washington, DC 20035
202-332-2276

HEALTH CARE POWERS OF ATTORNEY AND LIVING WILLS

People are entitled to decide what kind of medical care and extraordinary measures they want in the event of a catastrophic illness, such as an accident, stroke, aneurysm, heart attack, or other life-threatening condition. Each state and the District of Columbia have laws recognizing one's right to decide his or her fate (*living will*) and to appoint an agent to direct the medical care if the patient is physically or mentally incapacitated (*health care power of attorney*). Some states have a uniform living will and durable power of attorney for health care. Other states have their own forms and requirements. These documents provide an outline of powers, but not every situation is covered. A good website to visit for more information on this topic is at **www.estate.findlaw.com/ estate-planning/living-wills.html**.

Choosing the Right Person

The person who has been selected to be the agent for the power of attorney should be advised of the responsibility. The person making the appointment should discuss this with the agent well ahead of the time it might be needed. Make certain that this person will follow your instructions and beliefs, and not his or her own. Some people do not want to be responsible for another's life, so pick a friend or a relative who knows you and your wishes, and is comfortable with the responsibility. The agent designated for the health care power of attorney should have a copy of the living will and the power of attorney.

When you are hospitalized, the admissions office will ask for a copy of your health care power of attorney and living will, or for the name of the person holding these documents for you. Let friends and family know if you will be undergoing surgery or will be admitted to the hospital. If you have these documents prepared and available, your wishes must be honored.

PHARMACY OR PRESCRIPTION COMPLAINTS

Some managed care companies often require patients to use mail-order pharmacies, which makes it difficult to talk to a pharmacist. Orders are sometimes lost, drugs are sent from different locations around the country once your prescription is entered, and you could wait weeks for your order. If you need your medication, you have to pay full price at a local pharmacy. If this happens to you, save your receipt. Contact your insurance company and insist that they reimburse you for this expense.

Each state has a department to regulate pharmacies and pharmacists. Contact your state agency for more information or to file a complaint.

FAIR DEBT COLLECTION PRACTICES ACT

If you have outstanding medical bills, there are laws available to provide relief from abusive debt collection under the federal *Fair Debt Collection Practices Act*, which establishes the guidelines that those trying to collect a debt must follow in their contact with you. Under the Act, debt collectors must identify themselves as such when they call, and may not contact you before 8 a.m. or after 9 p.m. They may not call you repeatedly, or harass, oppress, or abuse you. They may not threaten to or actually use violence to collect a debt. You can instruct a debt collector to not call you again and they must abide by your request. They can, however, contact you by mail regarding the status of your account. (See Chapter 5 for more information.)

TAKING ACTION—STEP-BY-STEP

1. First, discuss your problem with your doctor. If this is a hospital or nursing home problem, speak with the head nurse. There may be a patient advocate or ombudsman whose job is to assist patients with hospital bureaucracy and problems.

2. If this does not resolve the problem, contact the head of the hospital or the nursing vice president. State your problem concisely and always keep records.

3. If you have a billing problem, contact the head of the patient accounts department.

4. If the safety of a patient is the issue, file a complaint with the regulatory agency that licenses doctors, nurses, or hospitals in your state. Nursing home problems should be reported promptly to the state agency or local health department. States are required to have an agency to assist senior citizens. Many local agencies exist to help seniors. Contact these agencies for help—they can be quite effective.

5. For a privacy complaint, contact the privacy officer at your doctor's office or hospital. The doctor, hospital, or other health provider must give you this information. The privacy officer should try to resolve the complaint. If not, file a complaint with the federal Department of Health and Human Services.

Letter 7.1:
Doctor's Office—
Violation of Privacy

John Doe
10 Pleasant Street
Sick Bay, OH 11111
456-123-4567

July 1, 2007

Privacy Officer
Doc Friendly, MD
4 Medical Center Drive
Get Well, OH 40800

Re: Violation of Privacy

Dear Privacy Officer:

Please be advised that I am filing a formal complaint with you concerning a violation of my right to privacy granted by the federal Health Insurance Portability and Accountability Act of 1996 (HIPAA).

On my recent visit for diabetic care at your office, the following problems occurred.

1. Your receptionist called my name in the waiting room and asked me the reason for my visit in front of the entire room.
2. While waiting to see the doctor in an examination room, my file was placed in a pocket on the door with my name and reason for my visit prominently displayed.
3. On my way out, the receptionist stated loudly that I needed to return to see the doctor in three weeks to check if my diabetes was under control. She also read off my insurance coverage and stated the balance I owed in front of the entire waiting room.

These incidents humiliated me. I do not wish to share my personal information with anyone other than those necessary.

Please address these issues.

Very truly yours,

John Doe

Letter 7.2:
Doctor's Office—Violation of Privacy;
Second Letter

John Doe
10 Pleasant Street
Sick Bay, OH 11111
456-123-4567

July 15, 2007

Privacy Officer
Doc Friendly, MD
4 Medical Center Drive
Get Well, OH 40800

Re: Violation of Privacy

Dear Privacy Officer:

I have not yet received any information from you about my rights under the section of HIPAA federal law effective April 14, 2003. Please send me a copy of your privacy notice for patients.

Thank you,

John Doe

Letter 7.3:
Department of Health—
Violation of Privacy; Follow-Up Letter

John Doe
10 Pleasant Street
Sick Bay, OH 11111
456-123-4567

August 15, 2007

Secretary
U.S. Department of Health and Human Services
200 Independence Avenue, SW
Washington, DC 20201

Re: Violation of Privacy

Dear Secretary:

I have tried to resolve various violations of my rights to medical privacy under HIPAA with my doctor, without success. Enclosed please find a copy of my letter of July 1, 2007, to the privacy officer at Dr. Friendly's office. I have not received a reply.

Please investigate my complaint.

Thank you,

John Doe

Letter 7.4:
Health Insurance—
Billing Error

Jane Patient
4 Maple Drive
Skokie, IL 62700
847-555-0000

May 3, 2007

Oak Healthcare Company
Member Services
1 Corporate Street
New York, NY 11111

Re: Member #1234

Dear Sir or Madam:

Please be advised that a billing mistake was made in processing payment for the enclosed bill from my physician, Dr. Michael Feelgood. You have paid him as an out-of-network provider, but he is a member of the network of physicians in my plan. He practices with the St. Elsewhere medical group at the address on the enclosed bill.

Please review the payment of this claim. I should not have any liability for payment, except for the $15 co-payment I already made. You should have paid Dr. Feelgood at 100% reimbursement instead of the 70% rate.

Thank you for your prompt attention to this matter.

Very truly yours,

Jane Patient

Letter 7.5:
Health Insurance—
Refusal of Prescription Drug

Robert Outofpocket
6 Nomeds Lane
Soothe, VA 55555
434-400-1234

April 2, 2007

Oak Healthcare Company
Member Services
1 Corporate Street
New York, NY 11111

Re: Member #458921

Dear Sir or Madam:

On March 22, 2007, you processed my claim for payment of Cellsept, a prescription drug. Payment was denied because it is not in your formulary.

I suffer from a very rare illness, Behcet's Disease, which requires the use of this new drug. A letter from my physician supporting this statement is enclosed. There is no other drug available for treatment of this condition.

Please review the denial of payment for this drug.

Very truly yours,

Robert Outofpocket

Letter 7.6:
Health Insurance—Refusal of Prescription Drug; Second Letter

Robert Outofpocket
6 Nomeds Lane
Soothe, VA 55555
434-400-1234

April 22, 2007

Oak Healthcare Company
Member Services
1 Corporate Street
New York, NY 11111

Re: Member #458921

Dear Sir or Madam:

I am writing to you to request that you reconsider the denial of payment for my medication, Cellcept, a new prescription drug. This drug is not in your formulary, but my doctor wants me to have this new pill. A letter from my physician, Dr. John Doe, is enclosed.

Please contact me at the address above, if you need more information.

Very truly yours,

Robert Outofpocket

Letter 7.7:
Health Insurance—
Claims Clerk Error

Amanda Veranda
12 Lafayette Place
New Orleans, LA 72110
505-333-2222

July 15, 2007

Dr. Aaron Ace
Medical Director
Cheap Insurance Company
3478 Smith Drive
Suite 1100
Cleveland, OH 223344

Re: Member #7777

Dear Dr. Ace:

I am writing to request that your company reconsider its refusal to pay for my medication, Remicade. This drug is given in the doctor's office or hospital via intravenous line. Payment for treatment has been denied because your claims clerk stated that pills are available at a lower cost for the treatment of my rheumatoid arthritis.

Enclosed please find a letter from my physician summarizing all the drugs I have already tried without much success. Remicade is a new drug that is proving very useful in treating cases of rheumatoid arthritis that have not responded to other drugs.

Please reconsider the denial of this treatment. I need it desperately.

Very truly yours,

Amanda Veranda

Letter 7.8:
Health Insurance—
Denial of Coverage

John Jones
18 Brummel Street
Evansville, IN 82304
555-555-1212

March 23, 2007

Medical Director
Tight Fisted Health Organization
1200 Main Highway
Indianapolis, IN 82300

Re: Surgery Appeal

Dear Sir or Madam:

I am writing to you to appeal the denial of coverage for my requested stomach stapling procedure. My internist has written to advise that I am 50 years old, diabetic, and 125 pounds overweight. You declined to pay for this surgery because it is cosmetic.

My internist, Dr. Stuart Sonshein, and my surgeon, Dr. Nancy Craft, believe that this operation is medically necessary. Their documentation is enclosed.

Your treatment guidelines available on the company website clearly state that those who are more than 100 pounds overweight qualify for the coverage of this surgery. I believe my coverage was denied in error.

Please reconsider your denial of this surgery.

Very truly yours,

John Jones

Letter 7.9:
Hospital—
Uninsured Patient

Uninsured Patient
18 Hardluck Street
Philadelphia, PA 02222
555-555-5555

July 14, 2007

Patient Accounts Manager
Franklin University Hospital
12 Freedom Square
Philadelphia, PA 02222

Re: Uninsured Patient

Dear Sir or Madam:

I do not have health insurance because I was laid off from my job over a year ago. My benefits have run out.

On June 5, I was injured in a car accident. I needed surgery and was hospitalized for four days. I recently received a bill for $100,000. I called your office to ask about the rates for care. Your representative told me that patients without insurance are billed at a premium rate.

You receive federal and state funds, and are obligated to provide care for the needy under certain circumstances. I believe that you should reduce the bill to the discounted amount paid by managed care insurance.

Please send me an itemized copy of the bill.

Very truly yours,

Uninsured Patient

Letter 7.10:
Collection Agency—
Cease Contact

Uninsured Patient
18 Hardluck Street
Philadelphia, PA 02222
555-555-5555

July 24, 2007

Ruthless Collection Agency
P.O. Box 600
Johnstown, PA 02300

Re: Cease Contact File #3080

Dear Sir or Madam:

Please cease and desist from contacting me to collect a debt allegedly owed to the Franklin Hospital for $100,000. I am disputing the accuracy of the debt. In any event, I do not wish to be contacted again about this matter.

Very truly yours,

Uninsured Patient
Via certified mail

Letter 7.11:
Hospital—
Unclean Facilities and Poor Care

Kirby Katt
929 Westgate Drive
Albuquerque, NM 04020
555-444-9898

June 3, 2007

President
Local Hospital
25 Southwest Street
Albuquerque, NM 04022

Re: Unclean Facilities and Poor Care

Dear Sir or Madam:

I was hospitalized at your facility from May 28–30. I was in Room 422.

The room was dirty when I arrived. Used towels and washcloths were in the bathroom. I called the nurse, but no one came to clean. I called housekeeping, but no one responded. My doctor arrived for rounds and saw the mess. When she addressed the staff, finally someone cleaned and provided fresh linens.

The dietary department never came so that I could order food. I did not eat for 24 hours because I was told I was not on the computer list. Each mealtime I called the dietary office and the nurse, but I was told the food was on the way.

Please contact me to discuss these problems.

Very truly yours,

Kirby Katt

Letter 7.12:
Nursing Home—
Lack of Acceptable Care

Baby Boomer
38 Mockingbird Lane
Onarga, IL 60300
555-555-1455

May 15, 2007

Administrator
Superior Nursing Home
14 Montebello Drive
Lincoln Way, IL 60305

Re: Betty Boomer's Care

Dear Sir or Madam:

My mother, Betty Boomer, is a patient in your facility. She suffers from advanced Alzheimer's disease.

When I visited my mother recently, I was shocked to see that she had bedsores, her linens had not been changed, and her clothes had not been changed. It was obvious that no one had bathed my mother in some time. I rang for help, but no one came.

Finally, I went to the nurse's station to complain. No nurse was there. An aide told me that the buzzer system had been broken for several weeks. She also confided that they were very short of staff.

This lack of care is unacceptable and dangerous. Please contact me to discuss this matter at once. A copy of my mother's power of attorney giving me the right to handle her affairs is enclosed.

Very truly yours,

Baby Boomer

Letter 7.13:
Hospital—
Life Support for Relative

Ann Adams
330 East Lake Shore Drive
Chicago, IL 60600
312-555-5555

April 23, 2007

President Rachel Cook
University Hospital
2000 University Center
Chicago, IL 60699

Re: Life Support for Leonore Adams

Dear President Cook:

I am a daughter of Leonore Adams, a patient at your hospital. My mother has been a patient at your hospital for several weeks after suffering a stroke. Her condition is poor, but according to the doctors, there is some hope.

The doctors say that life support is available, but not recommended for my mother. I believe that she would want to fight for life at all costs. I know that I want her to have every available opportunity to live.

My brothers and sisters do not agree with me. Please have the doctors start my mother on life support immediately.

Very truly yours,

Ann Adams
Via hand delivery

Letter 7.14:
Hospital—
Power of Attorney for Health Care

Jane Adams
2588 McHenry Square
Marengo, IL 60000
815-555-5555

April 24, 2007

President Rachel Cook
University Hospital
2000 University Center
Chicago, IL 60699

Re: Life Support for Leonore Adams

Dear President Cook:

Thank you for your letter concerning life support for my mother, Leonore Adams. I understand that my sister, Ann, has contacted you to demand that life support be initiated for our mother immediately.

Please be advised that I hold the power of attorney for health care and living will for my mother. Copies of these documents are enclosed. You will note that my mother did not want to have any extraordinary means used to prolong her life in the case of a stroke or other catastrophic event. We talked about this many times. She watched others suffer and lose their dignity during prolonged, unsuccessful hospitalizations.

My sister, Ann, has been estranged from the family for some time. She has not even spoken with my mother in years. My mother knew that I would respect her wishes, even if the decision is painful. Please place a do not resuscitate order on my mother's chart.

Very truly yours,

Jane Adams

Letter 7.15:
Mail Order Pharmacy—
Dispute Charges and Services

Marsha Monroe
894 Wilshire Boulevard
Beverly Hills, CA 90210
213-555-5555

April 12, 2007

Customer Service Manager
Budget Mail Order Pharmacy
P.O. Box 1200
Las Vegas, NV 22222

Re: Acct. 36322

Dear Sir or Madam:

I am required to use your pharmacy service by my insurance company. The quality of care is very poor.

As a diabetic, and I need to have a constant supply of my insulin and other medications. You have lost my orders or denied that I requested the prescriptions. I am often required to place the same order two or three times before it is sent. Many times I have run out of medication because of your mistakes. Then I am required to fill the prescriptions at a local pharmacy at a much higher rate. I am enclosing those higher rate prescriptions for reimbursement.

The prescriptions have been short of pills prescribed. My most recent order of Prandin contained 76 pills instead of the 90 that were ordered and charged to my account.

If this service does not improve, I shall complain to the state and federal authorities. I have already complained to my insurance carrier.

Very truly yours,

Marsha Monroe

8

Home

This chapter looks at many possible problems involving your home. Whether the problems involve legal issues between a landlord and tenant, mortgage issues between a homeowner and the bank, or just aspects of day-to-day living, many common situations are covered in this chapter.

Landlord/tenant questions are very common. How you can get your security deposit back, when your landlord can withhold the security deposit, and whether a landlord is required to accept a *Section 8* (government housing assistance voucher) tenant or not are all answered in this chapter.

Homeowners have special rights that they need to be aware of in regards to their mortgages and home improvements. These rights and others are discussed in detail in the following pages.

This chapter also includes an extensive explanation of the Do Not Call Registry, the wildly successful federal program that prevents solicitors from calling you at home. The rules of each state are included, as is information about where to sign up.

Finally, for members of the military, this chapter discusses your rights while on active duty. Your mortgage rate cannot exceed a certain amount, no matter what your mortgage note says. Your credit cards also cannot exceed a certain interest rate, despite what your credit card company tries to charge.

HOUSING DISCRIMINATION

The Department of Justice administers the *Fair Housing Act* (FHA). It is illegal for housing providers to deny housing based on race, color, religion, sex, national origin, familial status (having children under the age of 18 or being pregnant), or disability. Housing providers include landlords and real estate companies, as well as other entities, such as municipalities, banks, other lending institutions, and homeowners insurance companies. It is also illegal to refuse to rent or sell a house to a person with a disability, a family with children, or a person with HIV/AIDS or related illnesses. It is illegal to refuse to make certain accommodations for people recovering from alcohol or substance abuse, or suffering from HIV/AIDS-related illnesses.

Some local laws prohibit discrimination on the basis of source of income. *Section 8* is a housing program for low-income people. It may be discrimination to refuse to rent to a Section 8 tenant simply because the source of the rent payment is federal funds. Local laws vary, so it is probably best to consult an experienced landlord/tenant lawyer. Landlord associations or tenant advocacy groups may also be able to provide helpful information.

Federal laws prohibiting discrimination on the basis of source of income are enforced by the *Department of Housing and Urban Development* (HUD). The agency's extensive website is **www.hud.gov**. There is an online complaint form that you may use, or you may obtain a copy of the complaint form and mail it in or drop it off at a local office. The addresses and telephone numbers of regional offices are available on the website. The national address is:

Department of Housing and Urban Development
451 7th Street, SW
Washington, DC 20410
202-708-1112

SECURITY DEPOSITS

Most state and local laws require the landlord to return the security deposit if the apartment is clean and without damage, except for normal wear and tear. Usually, the landlord is required to provide an itemized list of repairs and paid bills to justify the withholding of the security deposit.

If you are a tenant, it is advisable to take pictures of the way in which you leave the premises. You should also try to obtain an inspection of the apartment by the landlord when you move out, so that you have a written record of the condition in which you left the premises.

SAFETY CONDITIONS

Property owners have a general duty to keep their premises free from hazards. An accumulation of ice on stairs required to access the apartment is possibly negligent. State laws vary about the liability for shoveling snow. In some states, the landlord is protected if he or she does not shovel the natural accumulation of snow and ice, but if the landlord chooses to remove the ice and snow and does it negligently, he or she may be liable for injuries.

If an injury occurs on the premises, the tenant should file the insurance claims, and should keep copies of the hospital bills and records. All correspondence and claims should be sent via certified mail. If the injuries are serious enough, consider retaining an attorney. Lawyers usually do not charge for personal injury suit consultations. They will collect a fee from the defendant if the case is successful.

PRIVATE MORTGAGE INSURANCE (PMI)

Most lenders require borrowers to have *private mortgage insurance* (PMI) in case the borrower defaults on the loan. The reasoning behind the imposition of PMI is that lenders believe that an owner with little equity is more likely to default on the loan. The *Homeowner's Protection Act* requires lenders to automatically terminate PMI at certain scheduled dates under certain specific requirements. It also allows for borrower-requested cancellation at certain scheduled dates. The Act applies to loans made after July 29, 1999, and excludes certain high-risk FHA and VA loans.

In general terms, borrowers may request that PMI be cancelled when the principal balance of the mortgage loan reaches 80% of the original value of the property securing the loan. If the homeowner does not request cancellation, PMI is to automatically terminate when the loan balance, based solely on the amortization schedules for the loan, reaches 78% of the original value of the property securing the loan.

If you signed a mortgage before July 29, 1999, you may ask your lender about canceling the PMI if you have 20% or more equity in your home. Federal law does not require your lender to cancel the PMI.

Fannie Mae and *Freddie Mac* are organizations that buy mortgages from lenders. They have regulations governing the payment of PMI. Individual states may have laws that regulate the payment of PMI. Contact your state's consumer protection agency or attorney general for more information for your particular situation. (See Appendix A for contact information for your state's attorney general.) The Federal Trade Commission (FTC) enforces the rules about the sale of private mortgage insurance. The website for this agency is **www.ftc.gov/ftc/consumer.htm**.

If you have PMI, carefully monitor the balance of your loan. If your property has appreciated greatly, you may wish to get an appraisal to prove that you have more than 20% equity in your home.

HOME IMPROVEMENT

Contracting for home repairs and improvements can be a risky venture. Most contractors and service providers will not begin working until a deposit is made or perhaps until an entire contract is paid in full. This leaves the consumer in a position of not being able to hold back payment for unsatisfactory, untimely, or incomplete work.

If you are in a situation where you have paid for work in full prior to actually having it completed, you have a few choices to resolve a problem of unsatisfactory work. If the company does not respond to your written complaint, you have the option of complaining to your local Better Business Bureau. The Better Business Bureau works to facilitate communication between the company and the consumer to help both sides come to a satisfactory resolution to the complaint. It also keeps records of businesses that had complaints filed against them. However, the Better Business Bureau does not have authority over the companies and does not take sides in disputes.

Going to small claims court is another option. Small claims courts are generally available in every state to resolve disputes, where the amounts in question are small. The actual amounts that can be brought in small claims vary by state, but generally have a maximum range from $2,500 to $5,000. Small claims courts are designed to be used without an attorney, so as to move quickly and more informally. Generally, there will be court costs and fees involved in just filing your suit.

Beyond these remedies, there may be other local or statewide consumer advocacy groups that can help. Check with your local government offices or your state attorney general's office to learn if additional remedies exist for your situation.

Cable Television Laws

In addition to the federal laws governing cable television, local laws may regulate your cable television company. Consumers have complained of missed service calls to their local lawmakers. As a result, many areas enacted laws that require the cable company to pay penalties to the subscriber for missed service calls and broken appointments. Call your town or city for a copy of the laws in your area. Ask your local reference librarian for additional help.

Utility Lines

The purpose of calling the utility service to mark the spot where the utility lines run before digging is so no damage will be done. The homeowner has the right to be fully compensated for any damage caused by a utility company neglecting to stake out the property. It is entirely foreseeable that a failure to mark utility lines can result in damage to the property. The homeowner has a right to have the requested service performed in a reasonable and careful manner. The utility company service should stake out the entire property. Utility companies can be sued for negligence.

If the utility company agent that was supposed to survey the property and stake out the utility lines was negligent, an insurance claim should also be filed with the homeowner's insurance company and the utility company. It would not hurt to contact a local council member or state representative about the utility problem. The local public utility board should be notified as well.

DO NOT CALL REGISTRY

The federal do not call law is regulated by the Federal Trade Commission (FTC). The FTC maintains a national *Do Not Call Registry*. Registration is free. Consumers may register by either calling 888-382-1222 (toll-free) or going online to **www.donotcall.gov**. Telemarketers must delete the names of those who have asked to be listed in the registry at least every ninety days. Registration is good for five years. You must call from the telephone number you wish to place on the do not call list. Cell phone numbers may also be added to the Do Not Call Registry. This Act also made it illegal to send unsolicited faxes to anyone who did not specifically request this communication.

Most telemarketing calls should stop within three months after you are registered. There are some businesses that are exempt from the law, including telephone companies, airlines and other common carriers, banks, credit unions, and insurance companies. However, telemarketing companies often make telemarketing calls for exempt businesses. The telemarketing companies must comply with the Do Not Call Registry, even if they are calling on behalf of exempt businesses.

The *Telephone Consumer Protection Act* does not cover political solicitations. Telemarketers calling on behalf of charities do not have to remove your name from their list, but you can direct the charity itself to strike your name from its telephone list. The charity cannot have a telemarketer call you after your request.

Even if you have registered your name on the national list, the law permits companies that have an established relationship with you to call for up to eighteen months after your last purchase, delivery, or payment to it. You can ask the company not to call again, and if the company continues to call despite your request, it may be fined $11,000. If you make an inquiry at a company or send in an application, the company can call you for three months afterward.

NOTE: *There are state and federal do not call lists. There may be additional penalties for violating a state do not call law. Check with your state. (See Appendix A for information to contact your state's attorney general.)*

SERVICEMEMBERS' CIVIL RELIEF ACT

The *Servicemembers' Civil Relief Act* (formerly the *Soldiers' and Sailors' Civil Relief Act of 1940*) is a federal law that provides active duty military personnel with certain rights and financial benefits. A creditor cannot charge a military member more than 6% interest per year. This is true for mortgages, student loans, credit cards, car loans, furniture purchases, and other consumer loans—even those made before the call to active duty or joining the military.

You must notify the creditor of your call to active duty. It is recommended that you enclose a copy of your orders or other proof of your duty status. If you are a reservist, you may wish to send a copy of your civilian pay stub and the reservist active duty pay stub to prove the disparity in your income. Send a copy of your orders to your creditor company via certified mail. If your orders are secret, then get a letter from your commanding officer or the base legal department stating that you have been ordered to active duty. The lender must lower your interest rate as requested immediately.

The creditor can go to court to try to prevent the lower interest rate. This presents another dilemma, because under the Act, members on active duty are immune from service of process and cannot be forced to go to civil court. It is unlikely that a creditor will challenge this law by refusing to lower the interest rate as directed. However, should a problem arise, military personnel should ask their base legal officer for assistance. Local bar associations may be available to assist you at no charge.

TAKING ACTION—STEP-BY-STEP

1. Review any written documents relevant to your complaint, such as a lease, contract, warranty, bill, estimate, correspondence, or deed.

2. Determine whether your problem is covered by the written documents, such as a lease for your apartment that requires the landlord to make certain repairs within a certain amount of time.

3. Research your rights under the law. These are written into any written or oral agreement you may have. If your rights are not spelled out in writing, you may still have protection under the state and federal laws, such as fair housing laws, deceptive practices statutes, and the rules and regulations of agencies like the Federal Trade Commission and Federal Communications Commission.

4. Send a letter to the proper person, company, and address. Keep a copy for yourself and do not send original documents unless required. Always keep a copy of any original documents you must send. If original documents must be sent, then send them via certified mail or express mail so you have proof that you sent them. You may wish to send the documents with a return receipt requested or a signature required for delivery.

   This letter should be brief and businesslike. It should not exceed one page in length unless you have a very complicated problem.

5. Expect to receive a response within ten business days. If you do not receive a telephone call or a letter in reply to your letter, then you need to move this to the next level of urgency.

6. Send another letter via certified or express mail restating the problem. It is okay to copy parts of your earlier letter if the facts are the same. You should add a sentence at the beginning of the letter in bold type stating, "I am writing to you for the second time because you have failed to respond to my previous letter, dated…" This letter should have a final sentence stating that you will be forced to take legal

action, including reporting the problem to the appropriate state and federal agencies, as well as private groups such as the Better Business Bureau, unless you receive a satisfactory response.

7. If you have not received an answer to the second letter within ten business days, then you must assume that the other side is not going to do anything to resolve the problem without being forced to by a court or other authority.

    You need to contact the federal and state agencies, as well as any private associations that may be able to help you. File a complaint with the local and federal authorities for a housing discrimination claim. Report a cheating building contractor who takes your money and fails to do the home improvements promised to the police and any consumer agency that may help you. Stop a collection agency from working in your state if it is not licensed to do business there—which happens quite often. Report a company that continues to call you after you have placed your name on the Do Not Call List. Whatever the nature of your problem might be, there is a place to file your complaint.

8. Hire an attorney to sue the offender. You could also take the other side to small claims court yourself if the case is not too complex. Each court system has its own rules limiting the kinds of lawsuits and the dollar amounts recoverable in the small claims systems. Some jurisdictions may require a corporation to appear through an attorney.

    The court clerk in your area may have helpful information online or pamphlets available to you explaining the small claims system. Sometimes local bar associations have volunteer lawyers at the courthouses to help small claims litigants file the papers. If you do not have the ability to maneuver through the court system on your own, ask a friend to help you or hire a lawyer. Most *pro se* (do it yourself) litigants do not know how to collect a judgment if they win their case. You may need to consult a lawyer after you win your case in order to collect your judgment or to enforce the action the court has ordered.

Letter 8.1:
Tenant Injured on Rental Property

Jane Tenant
1800 Ridgeway
Apartment 10
Wilmette, IL 60091
847-256-1212

January 16, 2007

Landlord Properties Management
190 West Randolph
Chicago, IL 60602

Re: Slip and Fall

Dear Sir or Madam:

I am a tenant in an apartment managed by your firm in Wilmette, Illinois. On the evening of January 6, I slipped on accumulated ice and snow on the outside back staircase leading to my apartment from the parking lot. All the lights in the area were burned out.

I slipped on the icy stairs and fell down the stairs. I had to go to the emergency room. My bills are enclosed. My fall was caused by your negligence. I expect you to pay these bills within ten days.

Very truly yours,

Jane Tenant
Via Certified Mail
Return Receipt Requested

Letter 8.2:
Carpet Company—
Contract Terms Not Honored

Craig Tully
9436 East 12th Street
New York, NY 20122
213-555-1212

February 1, 2007

Gotham Carpets, Inc.
333 Amsterdam Place
New York, NY 20122

Re: Carpet Installation

Dear Sir or Madam:

On December 1, 2006, I signed a contract to purchase new, wall-to-wall carpeting from you, to be installed at my apartment before Christmas. I was assured that you could order the carpet and install it before the holidays. As you can see by the enclosed copy of the contract, I stated clearly that installation must be completed prior to December 24, 2006.

The job was started on December 18, but not completed until January 15, 2007. I called, wrote, and visited your showroom to inquire about the lack of progress—but could not receive satisfaction.

I believe that you should refund $500 of the purchase price because you breached our agreement.

Very truly yours,

Craig Tully

Letter 8.3:
Cable Company—
Missed Appointment

Cable Subscriber
14 Monterey Drive
Chicago, IL 60600
773-404-1212

June 12, 2007

Cable TV Company
1111 West State Street
Chicago, IL 60601

Re: Failure to Keep Scheduled Appointment

Dear Sir or Madam:

This is to notify you that your service representative failed to appear at the scheduled appointment in my home on June 1, 2007 at 10 a.m. I waited until 2 p.m. and no one from your company came or called. I took the day off from work to be home when your company was supposed to install our cable system.

Under local law, I am entitled to be paid for a missed appointment. Please credit my account as required.

Very truly yours,

Cable Subscriber

Letter 8.4:
Utility Company—
Failure to Mark Utilities

Linda Homeowner
22 Charm Street
Winnetka, IL 60090
847-555-0000

May 1, 2007

Utility Clearinghouse
7345 Maple Avenue
Evanston, IL 60201

Re: Failure to Mark Utilities

Dear Sir or Madam:

Please be advised that I called your office to advise that I needed you to send out a crew to mark the utility lines in my front and back yards. We planned extensive landscaping. We needed to know where the utility lines were buried to avoid disturbing them.

On April 30, you sent a crew to mark the buried lines. However, only the front yard was marked. The backyard was never marked, and the landscaper cut all utilities buried in the back, including electricity, cable, computer access, telephone, and gas. I was out of town for the day and was not happy to return home late that night to learn of this disaster.

I called your utility line service in order to prevent this kind of damage. There is no excuse for this. Please contact me so that we can discuss a settlement of my damages without litigation.

Very truly yours,

Linda Homeowner

Letter 8.5:
Real Estate Company—
Discriminatory Practice (Race)

Home Buyer
90 Cobbled Road
Old Tyme, CT 40034
555-555-1212

May 2, 2007

Manager
Prejudiced Realty Company
100 Main Street
Fancy Town, CT 40085

Re: Discriminatory Practice

Dear Sir or Madam:

I am interested in purchasing a home in your lovely town. In April, I telephoned your office to inquire about seeing homes for sale.

When my wife and I arrived at your office to meet the realtor, he became very upset and flustered. Mr. Blow told us that all the places he wanted to show us had been sold in the past day or two. He suggested that we look in another area in which we had no interest. I believe that Mr. Blow decided not to show us these homes because we are black. He was unaware of our race until we met in person at your office.

I believe that your realtor discriminated against us on the basis of race. Please call me to discuss this or I will be forced to report this incident to the appropriate state and federal agencies.

Very truly yours,

Home Buyer

Letter 8.6:
Rental Company—
Refusal to Rent (Children)

Rose Renter
2200 West Grand
Apartment 860
Old Town, NH 01222
555-555-8999

April 8, 2007

Apartment Rental Management
P.O. Box 203
Old Town, NH 01222

Re: Discriminatory Practice

Dear Sir or Madam:

On April 5, 2007, I visited your open house to inspect apartments for rent. I liked your model apartment and asked for a rental application. The manager on duty refused to give me an application when he learned that I am a single mother of two children, ages 8 and 10. This is discrimination.

The Fair Housing Act is a federal law that prohibits discrimination against prospective renters based on many factors, including familial status. You cannot refuse to rent to me just because I am a single mother of two young children.

Please reconsider renting to me. Perhaps your manager made a mistake. I trust you do not have a corporate policy that refuses apartments to families with children. I prefer to resolve this issue directly with you, but I will pursue other legal remedies if necessary.

Very truly yours,

Rose Renter
Via Certified Mail

Letter 8.7:
Property Management Company—
Return of Security Deposit

Former Tenant
2 Greenbay Road
Kenilworth, IL 60033
847-256-1212

April 20, 2003

Landlord Properties Management
190 West Randolph
Chicago, IL 60602

Re: Return of Security Deposit
1800 Ridgeway, Apt. 10 Wilmette, IL

Dear Sir or Madam:

Please return my security deposit of $750, plus interest. I vacated my apartment at the end of March in compliance with my one-year lease. The apartment was clean and in good repair, less normal wear and tear. Your rental agent, Mary Jones, walked through the vacated apartment with me and signed the checklist stating that the premises were left in good condition. I am enclosing a copy of the signed checklist.

I am certain this must be an oversight in your bookkeeping. Now that I have reminded you of this, please return the security deposit, plus interest, to me at the above address.

Thank you,

Former Tenant
Via Certified Mail,
Return Receipt Requested

Letter 8.8:
Bank—
Cancel Private Mortgage Insurance

Betty Beisner
3065 Tranquil Drive
Muscatine, IA 20649
222-555-6788

May 5, 2007

Mortgage Department
Big Bank of Iowa
600 Main Street
Muscatine, IA 20649

Re: Cancellation of PMI

Dear Sir or Madam:

Please cancel my private mortgage insurance on loan #09213 for my home. The loan was signed on October 12, 1998. I have been a good customer, never missing a payment. I have about $25,000 remaining on the original $125,000 loan. The property is currently valued at $250,000.

Thank you,

Betty Beisner

Letter 8.9:
Bank—
Cancel Private Mortgage Insurance

John Homeowner
22 Wistful Vista
Anytown, KS 06177
200-555-5555

July 1, 2007

Bank of U.S.A.
Mortgage Lending Department
1200 Columbus Drive
Kansas City, KS 67388

Re: Loan #34909

Dear Sir or Madam:

I signed a mortgage for the purchase of a single-family home with you on August 3, 1999. The original mortgage amount was $100,000. I now have paid the loan down to $80,000. The home is currently appraised at $375,000. There is more than 20% equity in my home.

Please cancel the private mortgage insurance (PMI) on this property.

Very truly yours,

John Homeowner

Letter 8.10:
Business—
Junk Faxes

Local Business Owner
One Main Street
Any Town, IL 60155
555-111-4646

April 23, 2007

Bargain Office Supplies
1533 Sheridan Road
Highland Park, IL 60035

Re: Junk Faxes

Dear Sir or Madam:

On January 5, 2007, I received the first of many unsolicited facsimile messages (faxes) from your business. Your faxes are lengthy and frequent. They tie up my fax machine so that I am unable to receive customer orders and other wanted information.

You are violating the federal Junk Fax Law enacted July 9 of 2005. Each time you send me an unwanted fax, I am entitled to compensation of $500. Enclosed is a list of the one hundred faxes I received from you. Please send me your check for $50,000 by return mail. If I do not receive this check, I will take legal action against you.

Very truly yours,

Local Business Owner

Letter 8.11:
Company—
Remove Customer from Call List

Gerald Jones
3030 North Utica Street
Albany, NY 00000
234-555-8888

April 11, 2007

Ms. Nancy Pick
President
Ace Aluminum Siding Company
28 Main Street
Schenectady, NY 02345

Re: Do Not Call List

Dear Ms. Pick:

I am writing to direct you to add my name to your do not call list. I have also registered with the New York State list asking that telemarketers refrain from calling me at home.

Please make this addition to your list immediately. If I continue to receive telephone solicitations from your company, I shall take further action.

Very truly yours,

Gerald Jones

Letter 8.12:
State Do Not Call Registry—
Report Violation

Gerald Jones
3030 North Utica Street
Albany, NY 00000
234-555-8888

August 15, 2007

New York State Consumer Protection Board
Do Not Call Complaints
5 Empire State Plaza
Suite 2101
Albany, NY 12223

Re: Do Not Call

Dear Sir or Madam:

On August 5, 2007, I received a telemarketing call from Ace Aluminum Siding Company, despite the fact that I signed up for the state registry on April 11, 2007. The call came at approximately 2 p.m. from a telemarketer who identified himself as "Joe Jones." The telemarketing firm placing the call is Universal Annoyance Inc., a New York corporation.

Please investigate my complaint. The completed form is enclosed.

Thank you for your prompt attention to this matter.

Very truly yours,

Gerald Jones

Letter 8.13:
Federal Do Not Call Registry—
Report Violation

Alexandra Bell
10 Oak Street
Cincinnati, OH 02468
888-555-1212

October 17, 2007

Federal Trade Commission
Do Not Call Registry
600 Pennsylvania Avenue, NW
Washington, DC 20580

Re: Violation of Do Not Call List

Dear Sir or Madam:

On June 28, 2007, I registered my telephone number on the Do Not Call Registry with your office. I received online confirmation of my registration. Despite being listed, I received a telemarketing call from Annoying Calling Company about switching my long distance carrier. This call was received at my home on October 15, 2007, at about 8 p.m. The caller gave his name as Joe Blow. The caller ID showed the following number: 444-887-1234.

Please investigate this call.

Very truly yours,

Alexandra Bell

Letter 8.14:
Mortgage Company—Reduce Mortgage Interest Rate for Military; Second Letter

Military Homeowner
80 Cherry Drive
Onarga, IL 68900
555-555-2525

March 25, 2007

Customer Service Manager
Friendly Mortgage Company
P.O. Box 249
St. Louis, MO 63111

Re: Loan #69094

Dear Sir or Madam:

On March 15, I wrote to inform you that I am a member of the military called to active duty. I enclosed the necessary paperwork with that letter. Once again I have enclosed copies of the paperwork and a copy of my letter, because you have not responded to my request that the interest rate on my mortgage be lowered to 6% or less.

You are an FHA lender. Under the Servicemembers' Civil Relief Act, you are required to advise me of the adjusted amount due, provide adjusted coupons or billings, and see that the reduced amounts are not refused as insufficient payments.

The April payment is due shortly. I expect to hear from you immediately upon receipt of this letter.

Very truly yours,

Military Homeowner

9
School

More and more children are being diagnosed with disabilities from attention deficit disorder (ADD) to dyslexia. Each one of these children is entitled to a good education. The school must accommodate the student's disabilities. This may mean anything from tests without time limits to a personal aide for the student.

Students with physical, mental, and emotional disabilities are often *mainstreamed* (sent to class with other children). They are not always sent to different schools or classrooms, as they may have been in the past.

Federal and state laws govern the treatment of children with disabilities in the school. The parents or guardians of these children must be their advocates to ensure that all the services required are provided by the school. In special circumstances, if the school cannot accommodate the child's needs, then the district must pay the cost of another school for the child—even sending the child to an out-of-state boarding school.

INDIVIDUALS WITH EDUCATIONAL DISABILITIES ACT

The *Individuals with Educational Disabilities Act* (IDEA) requires schools to identify and provide special education to students with special needs. Once a child has been identified as in need of special education services, the school must prepare an *individualized education plan* (IEP) within thirty days. Specialists such as the child's teacher, school psychologist, special education consultant, social worker, and others prepare this plan. The school will invite the parents, and perhaps the child as well, to a meeting to discuss the proposed plan.

The school team should contact the parents to let them know the time and date of the meeting for presentation of the IEP. As a parent, you should have reasonable notice of the meeting. You also have the right to bring professionals with knowledge of your child's disability to the meeting.

After the school conducts an evaluation of your child, it may conclude that your child is not entitled to special education services. You have the right to insist on another assessment, conducted independently, called an *individualized educational evaluation* (IEE). The school must pay for this evaluation. You should provide a list of suggested evaluation providers to the school and try to get the school to use one on your list. The IEE should screen for all areas of your child's suspected disability.

If the IEE does not determine that your child needs special education services, you have a right to a hearing. At the hearing, you will need to have your own expert testify that your child has a disability. You should have an attorney well versed in school law to represent you. Several federal laws guarantee the right of a child with disabilities to receive the appropriate accommodations from the school, such as speech therapy, special aides, physical and psychological therapy, tests without time limits, and other benefits. State laws may also provide benefits for the special education student.

SECTION 504 OF THE REHABILITATION ACT OF 1973

The *Rehabilitation Act of 1973* is another federal law that prohibits discrimination against any student with a disability by any private or public school that receives federal funds. You do not have to wait to react to discriminatory conduct at school. It is your right under the law to ask the school to conduct a 504 evaluation.

Children with diabetes and other illnesses are often prevented by school personnel from participating in field trips and playing sports because of their special needs. This is often an unnecessary precaution that borders on discrimination. Students with special needs must receive appropriate treatment. For example, a diabetic student must receive extra time to finish lunch if necessary and be allowed to eat a snack as needed, even if the teacher does not allow eating in class. The medical needs of the student override the teacher's rule.

The American Diabetes Association has legal information available on its website, including a sample 504 Plan, containing information that may be useful to students with problems other than diabetes. The website is **www.diabetes.org/for-parents-and-kids.jsp**.

BULLYING

Bullying is a typical problem for students. It is not enough to expect the child to handle the situation alone. Parents and teachers must become involved. The students participating in the teasing and bullying must be punished. If the abuse continues, parents should file a criminal complaint with the local police. They should also demand that the school district pay for a private school for their son or daughter, since the school was not able to stop the abuse. If, after you attempt in vain to engage the school to solve the problem, contact the school superintendent.

TAKING ACTION—STEP-BY-STEP

1. If you believe your child has a learning disability or a problem requiring special services, ask the school to evaluate your child. Many parents already know their child has a problem—such as a speech impediment, depression, mental or emotional disturbances, or deafness—and may skip this step by providing their own evaluation by an expert to the school.

    NOTE: *If you ask the school for an evaluation for your child, the school must provide one.*

2. If you and the school agree that the child is in need of a special service, then the school must prepare an individual educational plan. Many schools are resistant to providing these services, so you must be assertive. If the school does not agree that your child needs special services, then you may appeal the decision to the local school board. Consider retaining an attorney that concentrates in school law to help you through this legal maze, because an appeal requires very specific steps, and you must follow them exactly or you might lose your right to an appeal.

3. If your child is being bullied, you must demand that the school deal with the bully immediately. Accept nothing less than a prompt end to all endangerment to your child. Demand nothing less than absolute protection for your child.

4. The bully's parents must be confronted by the school. The bully should be told that his or her behavior is wrong and forbidden. The parents must be told that their child will be suspended or expelled from the school if the behavior continues.

5. Complain to the principal if a teacher does not react to your concerns. If the principal will not respond, then you must complain to the school board, and then to the district superintendent. Complain to your state's superintendent of education, if necessary.

    NOTE: *Hazing, which has occurred among teenagers in high school and has resulted in broken bones and stitches, can be considered another form of bullying. Do not hesitate to contact the school regarding these situations.*

Letter 9.1:
Principal—Needs of
Diabetic Student

Concerned Parent
1900 Foothill Boulevard
Tarzana, CA 92159
213-444-8899

June 1, 2007

Headmaster Robert Chipping
Snooty Private Academy
32 Rolling Hills Drive
Beverly Hills, CA 92110

Re: Diabetic Student's Needs

Dear Mr. Chipping:

My son, Junior, is a Type I diabetic. He needs to eat at frequent intervals so his blood sugar does not fall too low and cause hypoglycemia. Junior's Latin teacher refuses to permit him to eat a snack in class. This is a problem because the class meets from 2 to 3 o'clock, hours after lunchtime.

It has also come to my attention that Junior was denied permission to try out for the school field hockey team. The coach told him that he was not a nurse for sick kids. Junior's doctor has given permission for him to engage in sports at school.

Junior's rights are being violated by the school. Please call me to arrange a meeting at your earliest convenience.

Sincerely,

Concerned Parent

Letter 9.2:
Principal—Screening Child for
Learning Disability; Follow-Up Letter

Jane Johnson
77 Sunset Strip
Los Angeles, CA 91130
213-333-7777

June 13, 2007

Mr. Osgood Conklin, Principal
Sunshine School
12 Education Street
Los Angeles, CA 91130

Re: Screening of David Johnson

Dear Mr. Conklin:

Please be advised that I am the mother of a second grade student in your school, David Johnson. He has difficulty paying attention in class. His teachers have complained that he speaks out of turn and disrupts the class.

I have spoken with his teacher, Mrs. Bradford, and with the counselor, Mr. Jackson, about the need to screen for Attention Deficit Disorder (ADD) or Attention Deficit Hyperactivity Disorder (ADHD). To date, I have received no response. I am now writing to you.

Thank you for your prompt attention to this matter.

Very truly yours,

Jane Johnson
Via Certified Mail

Letter 9.3:
Principal—Need to Develop
Education Plan; Second Letter

Jane Johnson
77 Sunset Strip
Los Angeles, CA 91130
213-333-7777

July 1, 2007

Mr. Osgood Conklin, Principal
Sunshine School
12 Education Street
Los Angeles, CA 91130

Re: Screening of David Johnson

Dear Mr. Conklin:

On June 13, I sent you a request to conduct a screening of my son, David Johnson, for Attention Deficit Disorder (ADD) or Attention Deficit Hyperactivity Disorder (ADHD). I have not had any response.

Please be advised that we have obtained a screening at The University of California for our son. Enclosed please find a letter from our expert, Dr. Rose Beck. She has diagnosed David with ADHD.

I want to schedule a meeting with you within the next week to arrange for the preparation of an individualized education plan (IEP) for David. This should be in place before the start of the fall semester.

Sincerely yours,

Jane Johnson

Letter 9.4:
Principal—Child's Right to
Individualized Educational Evaluation

Jane Johnson
77 Sunset Strip
Los Angeles, CA 91130
213-333-7777

July 10, 2007

Mr. Osgood Conklin, Principal
Sunshine School
12 Education Street
Los Angeles, CA 91130

Re: Screening of David Johnson

Dear Mr. Conklin:

On June 13 and July 1, I wrote to you to request that a screening and an individualized educational plan be prepared for my son, David Johnson. I have not heard from you.

Now I am exercising my right to have an individualized educational evaluation (IEE) at your expense. I want another expert in the field of Attention Deficit Hyperactivity Disorder (ADHD) to evaluate my son. I am enclosing a list of three suggested experts from local universities. Any one of these experts is acceptable.

Please contact me by July 15 to arrange for the IEE.

Sincerely yours,

Jane Johnson

Letter 9.5:
Principal—
Bullying of Child

Lawrence Reed
14 Exeter Lane
Boston, MA 33333
222-343-5656

May 31, 2007

Ms. Sarah Ambrose, Principal
Longfellow Elementary School
9009 Poets Lane
Boston, MA 33333

Re: Bullying of Betty Reed

Dear Ms. Ambrose:

I am writing to you concerning the ongoing bullying of my daughter, Betty, occurring in your classrooms. The problem has worsened since our parent/teacher conference in April.

My daughter comes home in tears nearly every day. She reports that the children in the 6th grade class tease her unmercifully. They call her names and pinch and scratch her. At recess she has been cornered and kicked by a group of girls. These girls also call her obscene names and yell other insults at her. The playground monitor has seen this abuse, but has refused to get involved.

Something must be done to make this teasing and bullying stop. I am demanding that the school act immediately. You, as the supervisor of these children, need to address this problem. The school psychologist and other professionals need to become involved at once. This is a very serious situation. Please call me to discuss the solution to this problem.

Sincerely yours,

Lawrence Reed

Letter 9.6:
Principal—Bullying of Child;
Second Letter

Lawrence Reed
14 Exeter Lane
Boston, MA 33333
222-343-5656

June 24, 2007

Ms. Sarah Ambrose, Principal
Longfellow Elementary School
9009 Poets Lane
Boston, MA 33333

Re: Bullying of Betty Reed

Dear Ms. Ambrose:

I have not had any response from you concerning the bullying of my daughter, Betty. Another school year has come to an end without any response from the school.

You are required to make a reasonable effort to resolve and accommodate my daughter's needs. First and foremost, you need to instruct the students involved in the bullying, their parents, and their teachers that this is not acceptable behavior. It violates the school code and state law. The behavior is cruelly directed towards a defenseless little girl for no discernible reason.

I expect you to remedy this problem before the start of the school year in August. This should include warning the children and their parents of the consequences if the bullying continues. The school code mandates suspension and expulsion of these students.

Very truly yours,

Lawrence Reed

Letter 9.7:
Superintendent of Schools—
Bullying of Child; Follow-Up Letter

Lawrence Reed
14 Exeter Lane
Boston, MA 33333
222-343-5656

July 1, 2007

Superintendent District 3 Schools
Dr. Nancy Foote
120 West Highway 11
Boston, MA 33333

Re: Bullying of Betty Reed

Dear Dr. Foote:

I am writing to you in a final effort to resolve the bad bullying situation that exists at my daughter's school, Longfellow Elementary. Previous attempts to rectify the situation have been fruitless. The teachers, the school psychologist, and the principal have not helped at all. Copies of my letters to the school principal have been ignored. (Copies of some of those letters are enclosed here.)

This situation cannot be allowed to persist. I am asking you to take charge of this problem immediately. Please call me to discuss this matter.

Very truly yours,

Lawrence Reed

10
Travel

Travel has become more difficult in recent years due to changing security measures. There are many rules to follow when traveling, especially by air. Check the Federal Aviation Administration (FAA) website at **www.faa.gov** and the Department Homeland Security website at **www.dhs.gov**, in addition to your airline's website, for current information.

DAMAGED, LOST, OR STOLEN LUGGAGE

The federal Transportation Security Agency (TSA) is an office of the Department of Transportation. Its employees are responsible for screening passengers and their luggage at the airports and elsewhere. The agency recommends that you travel with unlocked luggage, since it must be easily opened for security reasons. Recently, there have been many accounts of TSA airport luggage inspectors stealing from the bags they are supposed to be checking. In March of 2006, the TSA announced that two security screeners at the Honolulu airport stole $20,000 in cash from the suitcases of Japanese tourists.

In April of 2006, the Jefferson Parish, Louisiana sheriff arrested thirteen baggage handlers, including twelve employed by the TSA. They were charged with stealing from the luggage of airline passengers at Louis Armstrong Memorial Airport serving New Orleans. Items stolen include prescription medication, cash, DVD players, MP3 players, jewelry, cameras, and computer equipment.

The TSA does not advertise the fact that they will reimburse passengers for items lost, damaged, or stolen from their suitcases, but from 2003 to 2006, the TSA reimbursed passengers more than $736,000 for items missing from their luggage. For more information, including a claim form, go to their website at **www.tsaclaims.org/process.htm**.

The TSA promises that claims will be able to be processed online soon. Until that service is available, claims may be sent to:

TSA Claims Management Office
601 South 12th Street
TSA 9
Arlington, VA 22202
Fax: 571-227-1904

Lost or damaged luggage is a frequent problem. File your claim immediately when you reach your destination. Make sure your luggage is labeled both inside and outside with your name, address, and telephone number at home and at your destination. If your luggage is lost, but you are on vacation out of town, the airline will not be able to reach you.

The TSA has its own claim form for missing or damaged items. It is called *SF95,* and is available for download at the Transportation Security Administration website at **www.tsa.gov**. The telephone number for the TSA Contact Center is toll-free at 866-289-9673.

Be sure to get the names of the TSA employees at the airport to whom you report your problem. Get a written description of the problem and any information you can from the TSA and your airline. Take a picture of the damage when you get to your destination. Get written estimates of repairs or replacements.

PASSENGERS WITH DISABILITIES

The *Americans with Disabilities Act* (ADA) requires airline and security agencies to accommodate the needs of passengers with disabilities. The TSA has advice for passengers with disabilities on its website at **www.tsa.gov**. If you encounter any problems with TSA employees, file a complaint in writing by sending the details of your flight—number, airport, date, time of incident—and the name of the employee to:

Transportation Security Administration
Director Office of Civil Rights
601 South 12th Street
TSA-6
Arlington, VA 22202
Attn: External Programs Division

Diabetics

If it is medically necessary for you to bring syringes on an airplane, bring a copy of your prescription, a note from your doctor, and the box with the label attached from your prescription with you in your carry-on luggage. Carry the needles and the syringes with you, too. There should not be a problem.

TRAVEL AGENTS

The *American Society of Travel Agents* (ASTA) is a national professional organization of travel agents that has a consumer affairs department. The website for the consumer affairs department is **www.astanet.com**, and the telephone number is 703-739-2782.

The travel agency or agent must be a member of the organization in order for you to file a complaint. There is a voluntary mediation process. The American Society of Travel Agents cannot go to court or require an agent to reimburse you.

The complaint must be travel-related and less than six months old. You must have contacted the company first to allow it to fix the problem. If you file a complaint, it must be in writing. Be sure to include copies of your receipts, payments, and other necessary information. The complaint must be filed in duplicate. The Better Business

Bureau in your town, the police fraud division, or your state's attorney general may also be of service. You may also be able to pursue your claim in small claims court.

If the agency is bankrupt, all you can do is file a proof of claim as a creditor with the bankruptcy court. However, the chances of your recovery of funds in bankruptcy court in this type of case are very slim.

BUMPED AIRLINE PASSENGERS

The U.S. Department of Transportation administered Rule 240 governing the rights of bumped passengers. Each airline is allowed to make its own written version of this rule. The rule explains what the airline may do in case a flight is delayed or canceled. You may receive a free ticket for another flight, cash, or a refund of your money. Federal law requires airlines to pay bumped passengers double the face value of a ticket or $400, whichever is greater.

HOTELS AND OTHER PUBLIC PLACES

The Americans with Disabilities Act requires most public places to provide handi-capped access. Some hotel frequent stay clubs have a special number to call for prob-lems (check the back of your card).

If a letter does not bring results, then a complaint to the Office of Civil Rights and the local human rights agency should get some action. There are also handicapped advocacy groups in most major cities.

TRAINS

If you have trouble on the train, ask the conductor for help. The conductor is in charge of the passengers. The conductor may assist you in finding a handicapped seat.

Amtrak provides discounts for disabled travelers upon presentation of proof of disability, such as a doctor's letter. Contact Amtrak for more information, either through its website at **www.amtrak.com** or by calling 800-USA-RAIL (872-7245).

If you booked your train trip through a travel agent, then you may wish to complain to him or her. If that is not successful, then you could complain to the professional travel association to which your agent belongs, if you believe your agent was at fault.

Handicapped passengers must be accommodated under the federal disability law. The washroom and aisles should be accessible. There should be wheelchair-friendly ramps to and from the trains and train station. If your needs are not met, you can file a complaint at:

U.S. Department of Transportation
Departmental Office of Civil Rights
400 7th Street, SW
Washington, DC 20590
www.dot.gov/accessibility

TAXICABS

Most cities have taxicab services. A department of consumer services or a taxi commission usually regulates the taxis. This information should be posted inside the cab in plain view. If you have a complaint, start by contacting the city where the cab ride occurred. Complain to the tourist authority. Be sure to get the number of the cab and the name of the cab driver if there is any problem.

CAR RENTAL

The car rental business is very competitive. If the car you reserved is not available, then you should ask to speak to the on-site manager at the car rental counter. After speaking with the manager, if you are not satisfied, complain to the customer service department at corporate headquarters. The next step would be to complain right to the top—the chief executive officer of the company.

Many car rental agencies are franchisees. These are independent businesses that buy the rights to operate a car rental agency under the corporate name. The corporation may not have as much control over franchise operators as over its own sites, and the corporation may operate its own agencies directly. You will probably have better luck obtaining satisfaction from a corporate site.

If the corporation receives too many complaints about franchise operators, it could force the franchisee to sell its operations back to the corporation. Car rental companies do not want dissatisfied customers.

Remember that most people with standard car insurance do not need to buy the extra coverage at the rental counter. Check with your insurance agent before you travel to confirm that you are covered while driving a rental car. Take your car insurance card with you when you travel.

Certain credit cards also offer car insurance coverage for rental cars. Call your credit card company and ask for the current information about extra benefits available to you.

TAKING ACTION—STEP-BY-STEP

1. Read your e-ticket, paper tickets, or confirmed reservations. Be certain you are traveling on the right day and time before you leave for your trip. A common problem is travelers who misread their tickets and try to travel on the wrong date.

2. If you are required to reconfirm your reservations twenty-four hours or more ahead of your travel date, then you must comply with the rules. Many people are amazed to learn that their seats or rental cars have been given away because they failed to reconfirm their reservations before traveling. Always print out your reservations and confirmations, and take the papers with you if making arrangements online. If you reconfirm by telephone, always get a confirmation number.

3. At the airport, if your flight is overbooked, talk to the gate agent. You may wish to volunteer to be bumped. Be polite and talk to the agent calmly.

    If you belong to a frequent flyer group for your airline, try calling the customer assistance number for the group. You might be able to get a seat through the assistance of someone in that group. Some passengers have luck calling the 800 reservations number for their airline while they are in line waiting to talk to the gate agent. They can book a flight on the next airplane out or arrange to travel on another airline flying to the same destination.

    Additional help may also be available. Travelers holding certain credit cards may receive help from their credit card companies. There may be customer assistance available in a travel emergency, especially if you hold an elite type of card. If you have booked your flight or car through a travel agent or AAA, call the agency. Some travel agents and groups have twenty-four hour assistance available.

4. If your luggage is stolen at the airport, then you should file a police report and a claim at the airport with the airline and the Transportation Security Agency (TSA). There has been an increase in luggage related thefts in the past few years. Unfortunately, the thieves have been known to be employees of security companies, airlines, and the TSA.

Always keep a list of any valuables you may have checked in your luggage. It is best not to put anything valuable in your luggage, but sometimes it is necessary because of carry-on limits. Never put jewelry, cash, or medicine in checked luggage.

5. If your luggage is lost, file a claim immediately at the airport. Always have identification both inside and outside the luggage, along with a cell phone or other number to reach you in case the luggage is found while you are traveling. Ask the gate agent to provide you with cash for a change of clothing and a kit with toiletries.

6. After you reach your destination or return home, you should call the airline or travel agent to complain about a problem. If this does not solve your problem, send a brief letter to the appropriate person in the proper department at the airline or agency. The letter should contain copies of all necessary information, such as tickets, confirmations, and so on. Wait ten business days for a response. You will have better luck by tracking down the person who has the power to resolve your problems. The website of the company can provide useful information about whom to contact.

7. After ten business days have elapsed, you need to advance to the next level of pressure. Send another letter, and send a copy to any licensing agency or private association that may be relevant. For instance, if a travel agent booked you at a motel instead of the promised and paid-for four-star luxury resort, then contact the American Society of Travel Agents (ASTA). Wait another ten business days for a response.

8. After ten more business days have passed with no contact from the other side, then file a complaint with the governing agency, such as the Transportation Security Administration, U.S. Department of Transportation, attorney general of your state, or a private agency, such as the Better Business Bureau. If this still does not get you relief, then it is time to put this in the legal arena. Be aware that some companies may require you to submit to arbitration instead of using the court system. Read the fine print of your travel documents and car rental agency agreements. You may not be able to go to court. Retain an attorney or consider handling the case yourself in small claims court.

Letter 10.1:
Airline—
Lost Luggage

Ann Passenger
3 Middle America Lane
Dayton, OH 33333
222-222-2222

May 6, 2007

United States Airlines
Lost Baggage Department
Dallas, TX 02344

Re: Lost Baggage Claim #818909

Dear Sir or Madam:

Please be advised that I was a passenger on Flight 117 from Dayton, Ohio, to Chicago, Illinois, (O'Hare) on April 30, 2007. My luggage was lost on this direct flight. After more than five days, you have not found my luggage.

Enclosed please find my list with receipts of items I was authorized to purchase by your ground agent, Mr. Lennox. As you can see, the list includes necessary things such as underwear, clothing, and toiletries. The total is $347.76. Please send a refund in this amount to my address, listed at the top of this letter.

Please send me a claim form for the lost luggage. I would prefer to have my luggage returned to me.

Very truly yours,

Ann Passenger

Letter 10.2:
Department of Transportation—
Repair Luggage

Bill Passenger
44 Your Town Road
New York, NY 12345
123-455-6666

June 6, 2007

U.S. Department of Transportation
Transportation Security Administration
Claims Office
TSA Headquarters
West Building
8th Floor
601 South 12th Street (TSA-2)
Arlington, VA 22202

Re: Damaged Luggage

Dear Sir or Madam:

Please be advised that your inspector broke the lock on my luggage on May 25, 2007 at the airport in Palm Springs, California. The lock was open and did not need to be touched by anyone in order to view the contents of the suitcase. In the process of trying to open the lock, the fabric of the suitcase was ripped.

Enclosed please find a note from your inspector stating that the luggage was examined and the damage caused by this inspection, along with a copy of the repair estimate.

I expect to receive reimbursement for the full amount of my loss within fourteen business days. My claim form is enclosed.

Very truly yours,

Bill Passenger

Letter 10.3:
Department of Transportation—
Stolen Item

Fred Flyer
1903 Kitty Hawk Drive
Charlotte, SC 45023
222-333-5151

April 4, 2007

U.S. Department of Transportation
Transportation Security Administration
Claims Office
TSA Headquarters
West Building
8th Floor
601 South 12th Street (TSA-2)
Arlington, VA 22202-4220

Re: Stolen Camera

Dear Sir or Madam:

On April 2, 2007, I flew from St. Louis to Charlotte on Rapid Transfer Airlines, Flight 12. I checked my luggage with a skycap.

When I retrieved my luggage in Charlotte, my digital camera was missing from my bag.

I reported the loss of the item in Charlotte to the airline and the TSA office. Copies of the reports are enclosed. I am also enclosing a TSA Claim Form for Missing or Damaged Items (SF95) that I downloaded from your website. A copy of my receipt for the purchase of this camera is enclosed. I had just purchased this camera for my trip.

Please remit a check to me within fourteen business days.

Very truly yours,

Fred Flyer

Letter 10.4:
Department of Transportation—Failure to Accommodate Passenger with Disability

Caroline Smith
9214 Mulberry Street
Anytown, PA 74439
888-909-3654

July 2, 2007

U.S. Department of Transportation
Aviation Consumer Protection Division
Attn: C-75-D
400 7th Street, SW
Washington, DC 20590

Re: Failure to Accommodate
Passenger with Disability

Dear Sir or Madam:

Please be advised that I am writing to register my complaint about my treatment on Pegasus Airlines, Flight #2222, from Chicago to Los Angeles on June 1, 2007.

I am a passenger with a disability and I need a wheelchair to move more than a very short distance. There was no pre-boarding announcement allowing passengers who need more time to board first.

The gate attendant, Rose Washington, told me that the airline does not permit handicapped passengers to board first. I was also told I would have to walk to the gate. Finally, she told me that I could not bring my collapsible wheelchair onboard. This treatment violates the Americans with Disabilities Act.

Please respond at your earliest convenience.

Very truly yours,

Caroline Smith

Letter 10.5:
Department of Transportation–
Screening Discrimination

Barbara Oak
89 Monterey Drive
San Diego, CA 03810
777-062-4588

July 8, 2007

Department of Transportation
Director of Civil Rights
Attn: External Programs Division
Transportation Security Administration
400 7th Street SW, TSA-6
Washington, DC 20590

Re: Passenger Screening Discrimination

Dear Director:

I am a diabetic passenger who needs to carry my insulin syringes and needles with me when traveling. On July 6, 2007, I was flying from San Diego to Palm Springs, California. As I went through the passenger screening area, my bag containing the medication was searched and I was detained.

Although I showed the screener, John Jones, and his supervisor, Mary Bureaucrat, a letter from my doctor stating that he prescribed the medication, as well as a pharmacy label with my name and the medication on it, your employees confiscated the needles and medication. They told me that this was not permitted on the airplane. I fly frequently with this medication and have never had a problem.

I believe that you violated my rights by discriminating against me because of my disability. Please reimburse me for the lost medications, a receipt for which is enclosed.

Very truly yours,

Barbara Oak

Letter 10.6:
Trade Organization—
Travel Agency Theft

Rebecca Chase
300 South Thomas Street
Apartment 47
Reseda, CA 91339
818-609-0025

June 13, 2007

American Society of Travel Agents
Consumer Affairs Department
1101 King Street
Suite 200
Alexandria, VA 22314

Re: Travel Agency Theft

Dear Sir or Madam:

I am writing to complain about a dishonest travel agency, Fast Flight Company, a member of your group. On June 5, 2007, I paid cash for our honeymoon trip to Hawaii. A copy of my receipt for $3,500 is enclosed. This amount paid for five nights in Hawaii at the Surf Hotel in Maui and round-trip airfare for two, coach class, on Honeymooner Airlines.

The travel agency manager told me that the computer was down and that he could not print out our tickets and vouchers. He did provide a brochure listing our honeymoon package. I returned the next day for our tickets and vouchers as the manager asked. Imagine my shock when the doors were locked and a sign on the door said Out of Business.

Please reimburse me for my loss.

Thank you,

Rebecca Chase

Letter 10.7:
Airlines—Bumped Passenger

Bill Griswold
26 Sperry Street
Charleston, SC 10045
888-626-4876

February 11, 2007

Pegasus Airlines
Customer Relations
P.O. Box 12
Dayton, OH 24850

Re: Bumped Passenger Complaint

Dear Sir or Madam:

On January 2, 2007, I was a confirmed, ticketed passenger with a boarding pass for Flight #1800 from Palm Springs, California, to Charleston, South Carolina. I arrived at the departure gate one hour prior to check-in, where I was the first in line. I was bumped from the flight. I did not volunteer to lose my seat.

You rescheduled my flight for later in the day. The change in schedule caused me to arrive at my destination more than three hours later than scheduled. I should have received $400 in compensation, rather than the $300 you provided. The lower figure is double the face value of the ticket, but I should have received the greater sum of $400.

Thank you,

Bill Griswold

Letter 10.8:
Hotel—
Quoted Reservation

Anne Seth
83 Cross Court
Boston, MA 21377
515-293-1234

July 8, 2007

Premiere Hotels, Inc.
Customer Service Manager
77 Sunset Boulevard
Los Angeles, CA 91387

Re: Quoted Reservation

Dear Sir or Madam:

On June 1, 2007, I made reservations for two double rooms at your hotel through your website. The price quoted for each room was $125 per night. A copy of my confirmation with reference number is enclosed.

Imagine my surprise when my family checked in and was charged $300 per night, per room. I tried to show the reservations manager my confirmation information, but was told that such a low price would never be promised, despite the fact that the confirmation number was given by your corporate website. Please reimburse me for the extra charges.

Please honor the price you originally promised. I have always had good service at your hotels. I am a member of your Happy Hotels club. It would be unfortunate if I had to transfer my loyalty to another hotel group because of this incident.

Very truly yours,

Anne Seth

Letter 10.9:
Hotel—
Handicapped Access

Michael Brown
90 Westminster Drive
Spokane, WA 23245
909-256-4107

March 19, 2007

Manager
Very Fancy Hotel
700 North Michigan Avenue
Chicago, IL 60610

Re: Handicapped Access

Dear Sir or Madam:

I had a reservation to stay at your hotel the evenings of March 11 and 12. I made my reservation through your hotel's 800 number. At that time, I informed the customer service representative that I had a disability and required a wheelchair. I asked if your hotel is fully accessible at least three times before I made the reservation. I was assured that it was. My confirmation number is enclosed.

You could not provide suitable accommodations for me. I was forced to move to another hotel that had handicap accessible rooms. Please reimburse my credit card.

Very truly yours,

Michael Brown

Letter 10.10:
Hotel—
Misrepresentation of Facility

Jane Traveler
18 University Place
Memphis, TN 80956
555-555-1212

April 15, 2007

Manager
Family Friendly Hotel
900 South Office Park
Baltimore, MD 40933

Re: Misrepresentation of Facility

Dear Manager:

On February 5, I booked a spring trip for my family to your Orlando,
Florida resort. I booked the trip online at your website and confirmed
with your reservations office for a March 23–30 stay. I informed your
agent that my two children were ages 4 and 6.

I was shocked to check in on the morning of March 23 to learn that you
had rented most of the hotel to college students who were packed in four
or more to each single room. We were deprived of using the facilities,
except to bathe and to sleep, because of the rowdy behavior of other
guests. We stayed away as much as possible.

I believe that a fair resolution is to refund one-half of the charges for
our hotel room. A copy of the bill is enclosed.

Very truly yours,

Jane Traveler

Letter 10.11:
Railroad—
Unsatisfactory Accommodations

Ron Railfan
863 Robin Circle
Hoboken, NJ 12489
855-963-2087

June 2, 2007

Iron Horse Railroad
Manager of Customer Relations
P.O. Box 12
Horseshoe Pass, WY 12090

Re: Unsatisfactory Accommodations

Dear Sir or Madam:

On May 30, 2007, I was a passenger on Train #64 traveling from Detroit to Chicago. The rail car with my assigned seat was very dirty. A dining car was supposed to be operating during the trip, offering hot food and snacks. The dining car was closed. An employee did have some boxes of candy, a few bags of pretzels, and some cans of warm soda pop for sale. This was clearly inadequate for the hundreds of passengers on board.

This poor service is inexcusable. I deserve a refund of a portion of my fare for the terrible conditions on this trip. A copy of my ticket is enclosed.

Very truly yours,

Ron Railfan

Letter 10.12:
Department of Consumer Services—
Inflated Taxi Charges

Joanne Jones
103 Dobbs Street
Smalltown, WA
555-555-5555

June 5, 2007

Department of Consumer Services
Richard J. Daley Center
50 West Washington Street
Room 208
Chicago, IL 60602

Re: Inflated Charges

Dear Sir or Madam:

On May 28, I was a passenger in Cab #2200 with driver Don Cantdrive. He took advantage of my unfamiliarity with your city. What should have been a $6 cab ride from the Trendy Hotel to Navy Pier cost $35.

The driver also drove too fast and in a reckless manner. Please investigate.

Very truly yours,

Joanne Jones

Letter 10.13:
Car Rental Company—
Breach of Contract

Car Renter
38 Western Avenue
Portland, OR 84800
502-999-8888

March 26, 2007

Manager
Friendly Automobile Rental
Western Airport
Seaside, CA 91022

Re: Breach of Contract

Dear Sir or Madam:

On February 1, I rented a minivan through your website for a family vacation March 15–20. I need this particular vehicle to accommodate my family of seven. I charged the rental to my Visa card.

We arrived at your counter at the appointed time. Your facility did not have any minivans and did not expect to have one returned in time for us to use it. You did not have a station wagon or other vehicle suitable for my family. We had to squeeze into a large luxury car that was entirely unsuitable for young children. There was not enough room for our luggage. We had to hire a taxi to deliver the luggage to our hotel.

I believe that you should reimburse us for the taxi service for our luggage and reduce the rental rate considerably. We were at your mercy due to the demand for cars for spring vacation.

Very truly yours,

Car Renter

11

Products and Services

This chapter tackles common consumer problems not covered elsewhere in this book. Issues from unpaid rebates to gift card fees to unrecognized warranties cause countless problems for consumers. On top of these issues, there are miscellaneous consumer problems, such as telephone service problems, clothing that self-destructs after purchase, flowers that die after planting, and other annoyances. The list is endless.

RESTAURANT SERVICE

Poor restaurant service can happen at a coffee shop or a trendy, expensive restaurant. No matter how much your meal costs, you are entitled to be served promptly and pleasantly. The food should be delivered to your table at the appropriate temperature and cooked as you ordered. Ask for the restaurant manager or head waiter (in a fine restaurant) if you are not happy with the food or service. If you still do not feel like you received the service you deserve, it is time to write a complaint letter.

GIFT CERTIFICATES

Another annoyance is gift certificates and gift cards that have monthly fees deducted or whose value disappears altogether. State laws may require any unused property (such as the value of a gift certificate or gift card) to be deposited in the state's unclaimed property accounts. This has been such a problem that many states have passed laws prohibiting companies from charging fees to reduce the value of cards and certificates, or placing limits on the amounts they may deduct. The amount of money involved in restaurant gift certificates alone is staggering—billions of dollars per year!

REBATES

It is estimated that up to 40% of rebates are never claimed. This could be because the companies make it so hard to collect them. The following are some of the difficult requirements for rebates you may encounter:

- cut the original proof of purchase seal from the original outer box;

- send in the original receipt (no copies);

- send in a copy of the receipt (no original);

- rebate must be sent within ten days after purchase;

- rebate ended before purchase was made, but signs offering the rebate were still up in the store or online;

- rebate must be sent to an address that is incorrect on rebate form (you may be able to get the correct address and zip code from the postmaster at your local post office);

- rebate is available only to certain purchasers (such as first-time buyers); and,

- stand on one foot while rubbing stomach and patting head (just kidding—but with all the others hoops that must be jumped through, it sometimes seems like you have to do similar ridiculous things to get your rebate).

One of the most common consumer complaints today is in regards to rebates that are never paid. Some of the biggest names in electronics have been sued or investigated for failure to pay rebates. Everyone suspects that the companies offering rebates count on us never filing the paperwork necessary to claim the money. This is similar to the bride who sends out invitations to more guests than she can accommodate, gambling that not all the invited guests will attend.

WARRANTIES

Warranties are another source of problems for consumers. A *warranty* is a promise by a seller or provider to guarantee that the product or service sold will work, and it serves as a contract between the seller and the buyer. It may be oral, but is most often a written agreement. If a promise is made by the salesperson, get it in writing.

Warranties are implied when a sale is made. Two common types of warranties are a warranty of merchantability and a warranty of fitness for a particular purpose. The *warranty of merchantability* means that the item is going to work as promised. The *warranty of fitness for a particular purpose* requires the product or service to perform in the manner it is intended to be used. For example, a homeowner purchasing insulation for a home in Alaska expects the insulation to withstand very cold temperatures for long periods of time.

Implied warranties are effective for varying periods of time, depending on your state. An exception to an implied warranty is if the seller states that it is sold *as is*. The following states and the District of Columbia do not allow the sale of as is merchandise: Kansas; Maine; Maryland; Massachusetts; Mississippi; Vermont; and, West Virginia.

It is common for electronics and appliance companies to sell *extended warranties*. These are fraught with peril for the uninformed consumer. The cost of the extended warranty may exceed the value of the product. Consumers should note that it is common practice for a vendor to sell extended warranties. Most often, these are not warranties—they are service contracts. Be very wary of them. They usually do not guarantee replacement of anything, and charge you extra for parts, labors, and materials. Consider whether the seller has a stable and honorable reputation in your community. Will it stand behind your extended warranty? Take particular care with the purchase of items such as computers, televisions, CD and DVD players, music equipment (such as speakers), MP3 players, and other pieces of hardware.

Federal law requires the seller to provide the warranty information to the consumer before purchase. This warranty must be available in the store, on the Internet, or in a catalog. Read it carefully. Always get a copy of the warranty with your purchase. Does it cover ordinary wear and tear? Will a laptop be covered if it is dropped or coffee is spilled in the keyboard?

Consumers often learn that some sellers do not stand behind their products, cheerfully refund the money, or replace the defective product. As the old joke goes, some warranties are not worth the paper they are written on. Many of these warranties are virtually worthless because the companies do not honor them. That is called fraud.

The Federal Trade Commission (FTC) regulates warranties and other consumer problems. (See Appendix E for detailed information). You may also contact your local consumer protection authorities to report a problem. See Appendix A for a list of Consumer Protection Divisions for each state.

RETURNS

Stores have a bewildering array of return policies. The return policy at the same store can vary during the year. To make consumers more confused, the bricks and mortar store may have a different return policy than the online sales operation of the same store. Consumer laws in larger cities and some states require the store to post its return policy prominently. The online store should post its return policy. Do not buy anything if you are not sure of the store's return policy. You might be stuck with the purchase if you do not know the applicable rules. Some state and municipal consumer laws prohibit stores from unreasonably limiting a return policy. Check your local laws for more information.

If you have a complaint about a particular store, call the store and ask to speak to the manager or customer service department. Always be polite. If that does not work, send a letter. Be brief and include only the relevant facts, and do not forget to send copies of any necessary papers.

TAKING ACTION—STEP-BY-STEP

1. Know your rights under state and federal law. You must receive a copy of the warranty offered with each product or service under federal law, even before you purchase anything. In the case of rebates, read the terms carefully. Keep copies of everything. Send the rebate claim form via certified mail or via certificate of mailing from the U.S. Post Office to prove the date you mailed the rebate.

   If you have not received the rebate by the promised date, call the vendor and follow up with a letter.

2. Read the fine print on all warranties. Keep a record of them. Do not confuse an extended service contract with an extended warranty. It is very common and misleading for sellers to call the service contract a warranty. Most of the time, the seller is merely selling you service agreements. Be very careful when considering whether to purchase these agreements.

3. If you encounter a problem with a product or service, send a letter stating the problem and enclose copies of any necessary sales slips, warranties, or rebate forms. Be sure to tell the company what you want, whether it is a new machine, better service, or your rebate money.

   If you are unhappy with a restaurant, dry cleaner, or other service-oriented establishment, contact the owner in person. If you are a regular customer, the owner will want to maintain a good relationship with you. Do not use profanity or raise your voice.

4. Send a second letter if you do not receive satisfaction. State the problem again and enclose copies of any necessary paperwork. The tone of this letter should be reasonable, but firm. You may state that you plan to take legal action soon. Send the letter certified mail or certificate of mailing from the U.S. Post Office. Keep copies of your proof of mailing and any signed receipts from the delivery of the mail.

5. If you have not received a response or if the answer is not favorable, consider contacting the public relations manager of the company. The public relations manager may be able to cut through the red tape on your behalf. You may also consider contacting the general counsel's office. This circumvents dealing with clerks and sends the problem to the lawyers for the company. Always document your telephone calls and keep copies of your correspondence. Write down the promises made to fix the problem and follow up with a letter confirming the promised action.

6. Take legal action. File a complaint in small claims court or another division of the court system. You need to retain an attorney if the stakes are high. File a complaint with the federal or local agencies that regulate this industry. For example, if a rebate or warranty is not honored, complain to the Federal Trade Commission and your state's attorney general, your state and local consumer protection office, and a private group such as the Better Business Bureau. Be creative. If you are a senior citizen, then complain to the AARP or another advocacy group. Call your local newspapers, and radio and television consumer reporters. You could even start your own blog on the Internet to publicize the problem and to record similar complaints from other consumers.

Letter 11.1:
Poor Restaurant Service

P. Bear
8 Hundred Acre Woods
Rumbly Tummy, TX 75004
232-767-4545

July 30, 2007

Food Snob Inn
3088 Country Road
Gourmet, TX 00364

Re: Poor Service

Dear Sir or Madam:

On July 15, I brought a group of ten friends and family to your restaurant to celebrate my wife's birthday. The service was terrible. We had a reservation, but were not seated until an hour after the reservation time. Once seated at our table, we had to flag down our waiter to order anything. When we were able to place our orders after a great effort, the food did not arrive until two hours later! The waiter was clueless, addressing us as, "you guys." The waiter also made comments to us about our choices, such as, "You must be really hungry to order that much," and "That is really fattening." The requested birthday cake was never provided, despite repeated requests. All this cost me hundreds of dollars.

I believe you should refund the cost of part of the meal. We did not receive the meal or service to which we were entitled. A copy of the receipt is enclosed.

One of my friends, Eeyore, was very saddened by the poor meal. We were all disappointed.

Very truly yours,

P. Bear

Letter 11.2:
Restaurant Gift Certificate Not Honored

Frequent Diner
10203 Canasta Court
Great Oak, WA 80808
221-555-3456

July 15, 2007

Chef Bernard
Gourmet Restaurant
18 Fancy Street
Great Oak, WA 80808

Re: Gift Certificate Problem

Dear Chef Bernard:

I was delighted to receive a $100 gift certificate for your restaurant for my birthday. Tonight I invited my family to your restaurant for a birthday celebration dinner. When I tried to use the gift certificate, I was told that you would not honor it because the previous owner received payment for it. You purchased the restaurant on July 1.

This is not a good way to attract loyal customers. I was embarrassed in front of my family because you failed to take my gift certificate. I am not able to use the gift certificate, so my friends apparently threw $100 away when they paid for it on June 25. If you cannot honor this certificate, then the value must be escheated to the state or turned over to the unclaimed property division.

Please reconsider the failure to honor the gift certificate. We want to patronize your restaurant in the future.

Very truly yours,

Frequent Diner

Letter 11.3:
Gift Card Not Honored

Generous Grandmother
865 Sunrise Way
Mah Jong, FL 29044
445-677-8899

June 20, 2007

Office of Comptroller of the Currency
Customer Assistance Group
1301 McKinney Street
Houston, TX 77010

Re: Gift Card Problem

Dear Sir or Madam:

I am writing to you to complain about a problem I have with Scrooge National Bank. On December 4, 2006 I purchased a $500 gift card with the Master Vista logo for my granddaughter as a Christmas gift. She has not been able to use the card because when scanned, there is no value on the card. I believe that the bank failed to activate the card and to load it with the $500 I paid. Enclosed is a copy of my receipt for the purchase of this card.

Since last December, I have visited the bank with the card on at least six occasions. Several times I was told that I must have used it and that I am trying to cheat the bank. On other occasions I have been told that the bank made a mistake and that it would restore the value of the card after it investigates. Now it is six months later and the card is still not working.

Please resolve this problem immediately. Tell the bank to refund the money or load the card with the correct value.

Thank you,

Generous Grandmother

Letter 11.4:
Gift Certificate Expired in California

Surfer Dude
One Sandy Beach
Malibu, CA 99101
115-789-0101

April 1, 2007

Very Cool Wave Store
33875 Pacific Coast Highway
Malibu, CA 99101

Re: Expired Gift Certificate

Dear Sir or Madam:

I won a gift certificate in a surfing magazine contest. I was disappointed when you would not let me use my gift certificate to pay for a new surf board. I didn't understand what the problem was.

I checked with my mother—a lawyer—about these unfair and illegal practices. She says that under California law, you can't refuse to accept the gift certificate, because you did not put an expiration date on the card. Please honor my gift certificate and send me the surf board I originally ordered.

Thank you,

Surfer Dude

Letter 11.5:
Catalog Order Not Received

Catalog Shopper
250 Fifth Street
Milwaukee, WI 53009
203-353-8650

July 10, 2007

Lovely Lingerie Company
19 Simpson Street
Indianapolis, IN 64033

Re: Order Not Received

Dear Sir or Madam:

On June 12, I ordered several items from your summer catalog—order #180347. To date I have not received any of the items.

Please advise as to when I should expect this merchandise.

Thank you,

Catalog Shopper

Letter 11.6:
Rebate Not Received

Computer Geek
9071 Transistor Way
Wired, LA 85092
333-000-1212

May 14, 2007

Big Electronics Company
One Online Road
Silicon Valley, CA 92033

Re: No Rebate

Dear Sir or Madam:

On February 11, 2007 I purchased a Super Fast Laptop Computer Model XYZ from the Big Box Electronics store in my town. I filled out the paperwork for the offered $100 rebate and sent it to you that same day. On March 30, 2007 I received a letter from you stating that I did not mail the form by the deadline of February 15, and was therefore not eligible for a rebate.

This is not true. I sent the rebate material to you on February 11, which was four days before the deadline. Enclosed please find a copy of my Certificate of Mailing from the post office proving that it was post-marked in a timely manner.

Please send my rebate immediately.

Very truly yours,

Computer Geek

Letter 11.7:
Seller Does Not Honor Warranty

Jane Homeowner
12 Wisteria Lane
Cleaver, CT 20689
567-789-1100

August 12, 2007

Customer Service
Columbia Industries
4400 Dryer Drive
Heater, AR 40891

Re: Defective Dryer

Dear Sir or Madam:

On July 1, 2007, I purchased a new clothes dryer from my local dealer, Friendly Bob. I received a written warranty guaranteeing satisfaction, or a new machine or my money back within ninety days. A copy is enclosed. The salesman promised also that I would receive prompt service and guaranteed a new machine if there was any problem.

The dryer was delivered to my home on July 3. It did not work. The delivery people said they would be back with a part the next business day. They did not return for a week. After many telephone calls and a visit to the store, they did return on July 18, but could not make the dryer work. At that point, I asked for a replacement machine from Friendly Bob, but he told me to deal with you. Friendly Bob said his salesman had no authority to promise anything, and without a written warranty, Friendly Bob would not honor anything.

Since that time I have called and written to you no fewer than twelve times. I am so unhappy with your product and lack of service that I want a refund of my money. I plan to take that money and buy a new dryer that works from one of your competitors. I will not buy it at Friendly Bob! If I do not receive a satisfactory response within ten days, I shall have no choice but to take legal action.

Very truly yours,

Jane Homeowner

Letter 11.8:
Failure to Accept Returns

Frequent Shopper
20 Longhorn Drive
Dallas, TX 40439
999-777-1111

July 13, 2007

Needless Markup Boutique
1805 Prestige Boulevard
Dallas, TX 40422

Re: Failure to Honor Return

Dear Sir or Madam:

I am a frequent shopper at your store. In the past year, I have spent thousands of dollars there. Therefore, I am surprised that you refused to permit me to return a pair of shoes recently. A copy of my receipt is enclosed.

Your store policy allows returns at the full price paid within thirty days of the sale with a receipt. I returned the unworn shoes within fourteen days after purchase with my receipt. The saleswoman told me the new policy is that shoes cannot be returned.

The new policy is not posted anywhere in the store. I was not advised of this change in policy at the time I purchased the shoes, and it was not printed anywhere on my receipt.

Please direct the shoe department to accept the return of the shoes, or I shall be forced to cut up my Buys-a-Lot credit card from your store. I am sure you do not wish to lose my patronage after all these years.

Very truly yours,

Frequent Shopper

12

What to Do When the Letters Don't Work

You have been a zealous consumer advocate for your own cause. You have called, written to the offender several times, and if possible, tried to fix the problem in person. You have not received any satisfaction. Worse yet, you may not have received any response at all. Now is the time to call in the cavalry!

What can you do now? Slinking away in defeat is not an option. So, square those shoulders, rally the troops, and take a deep breath for your final consumer campaign against the other side.

COMPLAIN TO THE APPROPRIATE GOVERNMENT AUTHORITY

Do you have a problem with sales callers who do not respect your private time at home? Complain to the Federal Trade Commission and place your number on the Do Not Call Registry.

Has your health insurance company refused to pay a bill without justification? Complain to your state insurance commissioner.

Has your pharmacist refused to fill your prescription for antibiotics because he or she believes those drugs are overused? Complain to your state pharmacy board and the corporate headquarters of the drugstore.

Did your mortgage lender discriminate against you by charging a higher rate because you are a member of a minority group? Complain to the United States Department of Housing and Urban Development.

You get the idea. In this great nation, there are agencies that regulate almost all professions and businesses. Often, there are federal and local agencies that have oversight and regulatory powers over these professions and businesses. The agency can intervene on your behalf to resolve a problem. The agency may require the business to submit to arbitration to resolve your problem. An offending business can even lose its license or be forced to close.

The problem for the weary consumer is to navigate the vast expanse of bureaucracy to arrive at the correct destination. The consumer must figure out where to complain. Filing a complaint at the wrong agency is useless. Even if you can decide what the correct agency is, you must file a complaint in a way calculated to get results.

Sample Complaint—Lemon Vehicle

Ms. Valley Girl, an 18-year-old woman, graduated from high school and bought herself a used convertible from her local friendly car dealer with her graduation money. She did not seek anyone's help, except from her friends, who advised her on the color of the car.

This venerable Latin phrase should be displayed in large, neon, flashing letters above the entrance to every used car lot: *caveat emptor* (let the buyer beware). The car salesman is not your friend. He or she is not interested in finding the right car for you. He or she is interested in selling you any car in order to make his or her commission.

Ms. Valley Girl signed a sales contract for the car and did not read the fine print. She bought it without any guarantees or warranties in writing on the sales contract. It was purchased on an *as is* basis. She did not check the vehicle history. She failed to have an independent mechanic inspect the car. She took it for a spin around the block, and did not drive it on the highway or at a speed greater than thirty miles per hour. The car looked hot to her and she pictured herself looking even hotter in it. When she drove out of the lot, it died on the expressway just a few blocks from the dealer.

She called the dealer from her cell phone and told the salesman the car died. He said that he was sorry, but there was nothing he could do. Then she called her parents for help.

Some states may have a period in which to return the car or a cooling-off period after the purchase of the car. You need to know your state's laws. Do not depend on a law to save you from your failure to be an informed consumer. Even if the law does offer you some protection, getting your money back is an entirely different matter. You may have to go to court to obtain any relief.

Ms. Valley Girl's mother had the car towed to their trusted neighborhood mechanic. He looked the car over and noticed immediately that it had water damage. Ms. Valley Girl's father checked the history of the car by tracing the vehicle identification number (VIN, a universal required serial number assigned to each car manufactured or sold in the United States). He discovered that the car was salvaged after a major flood. He also learned that the odometer had been turned back. The real mileage on the car was 150,000 miles, not 50,000 miles.

Ms. Valley Girl's parents first visited the dealer to try to resolve the problem. They wanted to rescind the deal by returning the car and getting a refund. The dealer refused to meet with them. The sales manager told them that their daughter was an adult and she signed a contract. It was not the dealer's fault that she was a bad shopper.

Next, Ms. Valley Girl called the Better Business Bureau (BBB). Not surprisingly, she learned that this car dealer had many complaints against it. The BBB informed her that because the car dealer was not a member, it could not do anything for her except to remind her to be more careful the next time she bought a car.

Ms. Valley Girl surfed the Internet for help. She learned that there are several state and federal government agencies that might help her. She contacted the attorney general's consumer division of her state. The attorney general had a website with information about many consumer problems, including transactions with car dealers. She learned that her state has laws regulating the sale of cars. There are so many complaints about car dealers that a phrase has been coined to describe them—lemon laws.

The naïve high school graduate found out that her state's lemon laws protected the buyers of new cars, not used cars. She was not prepared to give up yet. Upon further investigation, she learned that her state has enacted laws to protect consumers from fraud. Car dealers are required to disclose whether the car has been in a natural disaster, such as a flood or a tornado or a hurricane.

She also learned that it is fraud if a car dealer turns back the odometer on a car. She learned that it is a felony in her state to change the odometer of the used car to show lower mileage than it actually has.

Ms. Valley Girl filed complaints with the attorney general of her state. She filed a police complaint against the dealer. She filed a complaint with the consumer agency of her large city. None of this helped her to receive a refund of her money. She did get satisfaction in sending the car dealer to jail.

Ms. Valley Girl was determined to get her money back. She could not find a lawyer to take her case on a contingency basis (meaning no fee is due unless the case is won), because it involved a used car. In new car lemon cases, on the other hand, the dealer is required to pay the buyer's legal fees if the buyer wins the case.

Ms. Valley Girl decided to file her case *pro se* (representing herself without a lawyer) in small claims court. She went to her local courthouse to get the small claims information and forms. The clerks were very helpful. She asked the law librarian for help, too. He showed her the forms books to use to fill out her complaint form given to her by the clerks.

Having prepared the necessary complaint against the dealer, Ms. Valley Girl filed her papers with the small claims court clerk and obtained a court date. The court clerk asked

Ms. Valley Girl to fill out a summons for the car dealership owner and salesman. The summons is the legal document summoning the defendant to court. This provides the constitutional notice to the defendant that he or she is being sued and what the case is about. It also contains information about when the case is to be heard. The court clerk sent the summons out by certified mail to the defendants for a fee. (Sometimes it may be necessary to send the sheriff to deliver the summons to the defendants. Your court clerk will give you the necessary information about local small claims court procedures.)

The court date was not too long after Ms. Valley Girl filed her complaint in small claims court. The judge read her complaint and then asked the car dealer's lawyer if it was true. After hearing each side, the judge decided that Ms. Valley Girl was defrauded by the car dealer and salesman, because the odometer was turned back and they failed to disclose that the car was salvaged from a flood. The judge ordered the car dealer and salesman to refund Ms. Valley Girl's money and court costs. They were required to pay Ms. Valley Girl with a cashier's check within seven days or face a proceeding for contempt of court. Ms. Valley Girl had to return the car to the dealer after she received the payment. She had the car towed to the dealer, and then she cashed the check!

TAKE IT TO COURT

Government agencies will not collect the money for you in most cases. They are not equipped to sue thousands of consumer enemies individually. The consumer agency may try to intervene on your behalf or may file a class action suit for all consumers in a similar position. Do not expect the agency to act as your private attorney.

If your problem escalates to the point where you need to go to court, determine if small claims court would work for you. This is an expedited, consumer-friendly procedure. Many courts have Spanish and English documents available for small claims court. You must be able to speak English to navigate most court systems, and if English is not your native tongue, then you may be able to bring your own translator or arrange for a court interpreter. Most judges are very lenient in small claims court, so they may allow you to bring a friend or relative with you to translate.

If you choose to avail yourself of small claims court, remember that you must follow all the rules and be respectful to the judge and to the court system. Dress conservatively and appropriately. Do not wear jeans, sports jerseys, shorts, drooping pants, low-cut blouses, or other overly casual clothing. Speak clearly and answer the judge's questions. Turn off cell phones in the courtroom, and do not chew gum or candy.

Sample Complaint—Failure to Deliver

Alan Railroader is a model train enthusiast. He loves to surf the Web for O-gauge trains for his computerized digital railroad layout. One Saturday afternoon he comes upon an engine for his railroad. Mr. Railroader orders an engine for his model layout from a company doing business on the Internet. It says it is a secure site for using a credit card. The site has many testimonials from satisfied customers. Alan Railroader orders an engine for $250 and pays for it with his credit card. The vendor confirms his purchase and states that the item will be shipped within five business days. The website states that the credit card will not be charged until the product is shipped.

Two weeks later, Alan Railroader does not have his train. He has come home from work eagerly each day to find that no package was delivered. Mr. Railroader checks his credit card—it has been charged. He calls the telephone number listed on the website. It is an 800 number with a recording telling him he has reached customer service and to please call later. He calls the number again. This time he is placed on hold and then disconnected by the vendor before he can talk to anyone. He calls for a third time. The telephone rings and rings, and then disconnects him.

Mr. Railroader then sends an email to the "contact us" email address for the seller. Another week goes by and he still has no package. He has not received a response from the seller.

Mr. Railroader is now very nervous. He calls his credit card company to ask it to investigate the charge. The credit card company agrees not to bill him until they investigate the problem. The company will also contact the vendor for him.

A month passes and Alan Railroader still has not received his engine. He cannot get a response from the vendor, and the credit card company is still investigating his claim.

Alan Railroader decides to complain to the Federal Trade Commission (FTC). He has gone to the consumer help website for his state's attorney general. There he learns that many links to federal consumer agencies are listed. He sees that when a catalog or Internet company fails to ship the product within a certain time, he must receive a message from the seller that the shipment is delayed until a certain date, and he must be provided with the option to cancel his purchase.

The FTC has an online complaint form, which he completes. Someone from the agency is also a train fan. The FTC calls the seller to find out what the delay is in shipping the engine. The seller apologizes and says that the response to its website has been overwhelming. It cannot keep up with demand but is catching up on its shipments because it hired extra help. The seller promises to ship the package overnight at no charge to Alan Railroader. The seller keeps its word. Alan Railroader is now a happy man. Mr. Railroader notifies his credit card company that he has received the package, and it releases payment to the seller. Now everyone is happy.

FIGHT FOR YOUR RIGHTS

No one else will work as hard as you do to protect your money. It can be difficult to find your way through modern consumer life. You must be your own advocate. Do not give up. You worked hard for your money. Protect it by protesting the treatment by your health insurance company, getting a refund for shoddy merchandise, and receiving the quality of service you deserve.

A

State Attorneys General Consumer Divisions

Each state has a chief legal officer known as an *attorney general*. This lawyer is responsible for overseeing the enforcement of the laws of the state. Local prosecutors enforce the laws unless there is a conflict of interest, then the attorney general of the state may appear in court instead of the local prosecutor.

The attorney general of the state usually monitors charities and nonprofit trusts to make sure that they are not fleecing donors or using charitable funds for their own purposes.

The attorney general is a powerful *consumer advocate*. The more active state officers have excellent consumer information in areas such as nursing homes, elder rights, identity theft, and Internet fraud. Each state has different laws. Activities of the attorney general may vary by state.

Many states provide a form on their websites for filing a complaint online. Some states also provide such forms in other languages or different formats. Please see your state's website for more information.

Alabama

Consumer Affairs Section
Office of the Attorney General
11 South Union Street
Third Floor
Montgomery, AL 36130
Consumer Hotline:
   800-392-5658
   334-242-7334
www.ago.state.al.us/consumer.cfm
File a complaint online? Yes.

Alaska

Attorney General David W. Márquez
P.O. Box 110300
Juneau, AK 99811
907-465-2133
www.law.state.ak.us/department/civil/
   consumer/cpindex.html
File a complaint online? Yes.

American Samoa

Attorney General Malaetasi M. Togafau
American Samoa Government
P.O. Box 7
Pago Pago, AS 96799
684-633-4163
www.asg-gov.net
File a complaint online? No.

Arizona

Office of the Attorney General
Consumer Information and Complaints
1275 West Washington
Phoenix, AZ 85007
Consumer Hotline:
   602-542-5763
   800-352-8431(outside
   Phoenix/Tucson)
www.azag.gov/consumer
File a complaint online? Yes.

Tucson

Office of the Attorney General
Consumer Information and Complaints
400 West Congress
South Building
Suite 315
Tucson, AZ 85701
Consumer Hotline:
   520-628-6504

Arkansas

Office of the Attorney General
Consumer Protection Division
Suite 200
323 Center Street
Little Rock, AR 72201
501-682-2007
800-482-8982 (Arkansas)
Consumer Hotline:
    501-682-2341
www.ag.state.ar.us
File a complaint online? Yes.

California

Public Inquiry Unit
Office of the Attorney General of
    California
P.O. Box 944255
Sacramento, CA 9244
916-322-3360
Consumer Hotline:
    800-952-5225
http://ag.ca.gov/consumers/general.htm
File a complaint online? Yes.

Colorado

Attorney General
1525 Sherman Street
5th floor
Denver, CO 80203
303-866-4500
Consumer Hotline:
    800-222-4444 (Colorado)
    303-866-5189 (Denver)
www.ago.state.co.us
File a complaint online? Yes.

Connecticut

Consumer Protection Department
Office of the Attorney General
110 Sherman Street
Hartford, CT 06105
Consumer Hotline:
    860-808-5400
www.ct.gov/ag/site/default.asp
File a complaint online? No.

Delaware

Delaware Department of Justice
Consumer Protection Division
Carvel State Office Building
820 North French Street
Wilmington, DE 19801
302-577-8600
www.state.de.us/attgen/fraud/fraud.shtml
File a complaint online? No.

District of Columbia

Attorney General of District of
   Columbia
Consumer Protection Division
John A. Wilson Building
1350 Pennsylvania Avenue, NW
Washington, DC 20004
202-442-4400
Consumer Hotline:
   202-442-9828
http://occ.dc.gov
File a complaint online? Yes.

Florida

Office of the Attorney General
PL-01 The Capitol
Tallahassee, FL 32399
Consumer Hotline:
   850-414-3990
http://myfloridalegal.com/consumer
File a complaint online? Yes.

Georgia

Office of the Attorney General
Consumer Interests Section
40 Capitol Square SW
Atlanta, GA 30334
404-656-3300
http://ganet.org/ago/consumer_info.html
File a complaint online? No.

Governor's Office of Consumer Affairs
2 Martin Luther King, Jr. Drive
East Tower
Suite 356
Atlanta, GA 30334
800-869-1123
404-651-8600
www.consumer.ga.gov
File a complaint online? Yes.

Guam

Office of the Attorney General
Guam Judicial Center
Suite 2-200E
120 West O'Brien Drive
Hagatna, GU 96910 USA
671-475-3324
www.guamattorneygeneral.com/
   div-civil.php
File a complaint online? Yes.

Hawaii

Department of the Attorney General
425 Queen Street
Honolulu, HI 96813
808-586-1500
www.state.hi.us/ag
www.hawaii.gov/dcca
File a complaint online? No.

Idaho

Office of the Attorney General
Consumer Protection Unit
650 West State Street
Room B-20
P.O. Box 83720
Boise, ID 83720
Consumer Hotline:
    800-432-3545 (outside Boise)
    208-334-2424 (Boise)
www.state.id.us/ag/consumer
File a complaint online? Yes.

Illinois

Office of Attorney General
Consumer Protection Bureau
500 South Second Street
Springfield, IL 62706
Consumer Hotline:
    800-386-5438 (Chicago)
    800-243-0618 (Springfield)
    800-243-0607 (Carbondale)
http://illinoisattorneygeneral.gov/
    consumers
File a complaint online? Yes.

Indiana

Consumer Protection Division
Office of the Indiana Attorney General
302 West Washington Street
5th Floor
Indianapolis, IN 46204
317-232-6330
Consumer Hotline:
    800-382-5516
www.in.gov/attorneygeneral/consumer
File a complaint online? Yes.

Iowa

Consumer Protection Division
Attorney General of Iowa
Hoover State Office Building
1305 East Walnut
Des Moines, IA 50319
Consumer Hotline:
   515-281-5926 (Des Moines)
   888-777-4590 (outside Des Moines)
www.iowaattorneygeneral.org/consumer
File a complaint online? Yes.

Kansas

Office of Attorney General of Kansas
Consumer Protection/Antitrust Division
120 SW 10th Street
2nd Floor
Topeka, KS 66612
785-296-3751
Consumer Hotline:
   800-432-2310
www.kansas.gov/ksag/Divisions/
   Consumer
File a complaint online? Yes.

Kentucky

Office of Attorney General
Consumer Protection Division
1024 Capital Center Drive
Frankfort, KY 40601
Consumer Hotline:
   888-432-9257
http://ag.ky.gov/consumer
File a complaint online? No.

Louisiana

Office of the Attorney General
Consumer Protection Section
P.O. Box 94005
Baton Rouge, LA 70804
800-351-4889
225-326-6465 (Baton Rouge)
www.ag.state.la.us
File a complaint online? No.

Maine

Attorney General's Consumer
   Information and Mediation Service
6 State House Station
Augusta, ME 04333
207-626-8849
www.maine.gov/ag/?r=protection
File a complaint online? No.

Maryland

Office of the Attorney General
200 St. Paul Place
Baltimore, MD 21202
Consumer Hotline:
   410-528-8662
   888-743-0023
www.oag.state.md.us/Consumer
File a complaint online? Yes.

Baltimore

Consumer Protection Division
200 St. Paul Place
16th Floor
Baltimore, MD 21202
410-528-8662

Eastern Shore Office

Consumer Protection Division
201 Baptist Street
Suite 30
Salisbury, MD 21801
410-713-3620

Western Shore Office

Consumer Protection Division
44 North Potomac Street
Suite 104
Hagerstown, MD 21740
301-791-4780

Massachusetts

Office of the Attorney General
Consumer Complaint Form
Consumer Complaint and Information
   Section
One Ashburton Place
Boston, MA 02108
617-727-2200
Consumer Hotline:
   617-727-8400
www.ago.state.ma.us
File a complaint online? No.

Michigan

Michigan Department of Attorney
   General
Consumer Protection Division
P.O. Box 30213
Lansing, MI 48909
517-373-1140
Consumer Hotline:
   877-765-8388
www.michigan.gov/ag
File a complaint online? Yes.

Minnesota

Office of Minnesota Attorney General
1400 Bremer Tower
445 Minnesota Street
St. Paul, MN 55101
Consumer Hotline:
  651-296-3353
  800-657-3787
www.ag.state.mn.us/consumer
File a complaint online? No.

Mississippi

Consumer Protection Division
Office of the Attorney General
P.O. Box 22947
Jackson, MS 39225
601-359-4230
800-281-4418 (in Mississippi)
www.ago.state.ms.us/divisions/consumer
File a complaint online? No.

Missouri

Attorney General's Office
Consumer Protection Unit
P.O. Box 899
Jefferson City, MO 65102
Consumer Hotline:
  800-392-8222
www.ago.mo.gov/consumercomplaint.htm
File a complaint online? Yes.

Montana

Office of Consumer Protection
1219 8th Avenue
P.O. Box 200151
Helena, MT 59620
Consumer Hotline:
  406-444-4500
  800-481-6896
www.doj.mt.gov/consumer
File a complaint online? No.

Nebraska

Attorney General of Nebraska
Consumer Protection Division
2115 State Capitol
Lincoln, NE 68509
402-471-2682
800-727-6432
www.ago.state.ne.us
File a complaint online? Yes.

Nevada

Office of the Attorney General Nevada
  Department of Justice
Bureau of Consumer Protection
100 North Carson Street
Carson City, NV 89701
Consumer Hotline:
  800-266-8688
http://ag.state.nv.us/menu/action_bttn/
  bcp/filing_complaint.htm
File a complaint online? No.

Las Vegas

Office of the Attorney General Nevada
    Department of Justice
Bureau of Consumer Protection
555 East Washington Avenue
Suite 3900
Las Vegas, NV 89101

New Hampshire

Consumer Protection and Antitrust
    Bureau
33 Capitol Street
Concord, NH 03301
888-468-4454
603-271-3641
www.state.nh.us/nhdoj/consumer
File a complaint online? No.

New Jersey

124 Halsey Street
Newark, NJ 07102
Consumer Hotline:
    973-504-6200
    800-242-5846 (New Jersey)
www.state.nj.us/lps/ca/dcapub.htm
File a complaint online? No.

New Mexico

Attorney General of New Mexico
Consumer Protection Division
P.O. Drawer 1508
Santa Fe, NM 87504
Consumer Hotline:
    800-678-1508
    505-827-6060
    505-222-9000 (Albuquerque)
www.ago.state.nm.us/divs/cons/cons.htm
File a complaint online? No.

New York

Office of the Attorney General
Bureau of Consumer Frauds and
    Protection
120 Broadway
3rd Floor
New York, NY 10271
Consumer Hotline:
    800-771-7755
www.oag.state.ny.us/complaints/
    complaints.html
File a complaint online? Yes.

North Carolina

North Carolina Attorney General
Department of Justice
9001 Mail Service Center
Raleigh, NC 27699
919-716-6000 (outside NC)
Consumer Hotline:
  877-5-NO-SCAM
www.ncdoj.com/consumerprotection/
  cp_about.jsp
File a complaint online? No.

North Dakota

Office of Attorney General of North
  Dakota
Consumer Protection Division
4205 State Street
P.O. Box 1054
Bismarck, ND 58502
Consumer Hotline:
  701-328-3404
  800-472-2600
www.ag.state.nd.us/CPAT/CPAT.htm
File a complaint online? No.

Commonwealth of the Northern Mariana Islands

Office of the Attorney General
Attn: Consumer Counsel
Capitol Hill
Caller Box 10007
Saipan, MP 96950
670-664-2341
www.cnmiago.gov.mp
File a complaint online? No.

Ohio

Consumer Protection Section
Attorney General State of Ohio
30 East Broad Street
14th Floor
Columbus, OH 43215
Consumer Hotline:
  800-282-0515 (in Ohio only)
  614-466-4986
www.ag.state.oh.us/citizen/consumer
File a complaint online? Yes.

Oklahoma

Office of the Attorney General
4545 North Lincoln Boulevard
#260
Oklahoma City, OK 73105
405-521-3921 (Oklahoma City)
918-581-2885 (Tulsa)
www.oag.state.ok.us/oagweb.nsf
File a complaint online? No.

Oregon

Oregon Department of Justice
Financial Fraud/Consumer Protection
   Section
1162 Court Street, NE
Salem, OR 97301
Consumer Hotline:
   877-877-9392
   503-378-4320 (Salem)
   503-229-5576 (Portland)
www.doj.state.or.us/finfraud
File a complaint online? Yes.

Pennsylvania

Office of Attorney General
Bureau of Consumer Protection
14th Floor
Strawberry Square
Harrisburg, PA 17120
Consumer Hotline:
   800-441-2555
www.attorneygeneral.gov/
   consumers.aspx?id=451
File a complaint online? Yes.

Rhode Island

Consumer Protection Unit
Department of Attorney General of
   Rhode Island
150 South Main Street
Providence, RI 02903
401-274-4400
www.riag.state.ri.us/civil/
   unit.php?nam=consumer
File a complaint online? No.

South Carolina

Consumer Complaint
South Carolina Department of
    Consumer Affairs
3600 Forest Drive
3rd Floor
P.O. Box 5757
Columbia, SC 29250
803-734-4200
800-922-1594 (South Carolina)
www.scconsumer.gov
File a complaint online? Yes.

South Dakota

Office of Attorney General South
    Dakota
Division of Consumer Protection
1302 East Highway 14
Suite 3
Pierre, SD 57501
Consumer Hotline:
    800-300-1986 (South Dakota)
    605-773-4400
www.state.sd.us/attorney/office/divisions/
    consumer
File a complaint online? Yes.

Tennessee

Consumer Affairs
500 James Robertson Parkway
5th Floor
Nashville, TN 37243
615-741-1671
615-741-4737
800-342-8385
www.attorneygeneral.state.tn.us/cpro/
    cpro.htm
File a complaint online? No.

Texas

Office of Attorney General
P.O. Box 12548
Austin, TX 78711
Consumer Hotline:
    800-621-0508
www.oag.state.tx.us/consumer/
    consumer.shtml
File a complaint online? Yes.

Utah

Division of Consumer Protection
Heber M. Wells Building
2nd Floor
160 East 300 South
SM 146704
Salt Lake City, UT 84114
801-536-6601
800-721-7233 (Utah)
http://attorneygeneral.utah.gov/
    fraud.html
File a complaint online? No.

Vermont

Consumer Assistance Program
206 Morrill Hall, UVM
Burlington, VT 05405
Consumer Hotline:
    802-656-3183
    800-649-2424 (Vermont)
www.atg.state.vt.us/display.php?smod=
    119
File a complaint online? No.

Virginia

Office of Consumer Affairs
P.O. Box 1163
Richmond, VA 23218
Consumer Hotline:
    800-552-9963 (Virginia)
    804-786-2042
www.vdacs.virginia.gov/consumers/
    index.html
File a complaint online? No.
Note: *City of Alexandria, Fairfax
    County, and Virginia Beach have
    their own consumer agencies.*

Washington

1125 Washington Street, SE
P.O. Box 40100
Olympia, WA 98504
Consumer Hotline:
    800-551-4636
www.atg.wa.gov/consumerintro.shtml
File a complaint online? Yes.

West Virginia

Office of the West Virginia Attorney
  General
Consumer Protection/Antitrust Division
P.O. Box 1789
Charleston, WV 25326
304-558-8986
Consumer Hotline:
  800-368-8808
www.wvago.us
File a complaint online? No.

Wisconsin

Department of Agriculture Trade &
  Consumer Protection
Consumer Information Center
P.O. Box 8911
Madison, WI 53708
608-266-1852
Consumer Hotline:
  800-422-7128
www.doj.state.wi.us/dls/ConsProt/
  newcp.asp
File a complaint online? Yes.

Wyoming

Consumer Protection Unit
123 State Capitol
Cheyenne, WY 82002
800-422-7128
608-224-4953
Consumer Hotline:
  800-438-5799
  307-777-7874
http://attorneygeneral.state.wy.us/
  consumer.htm
File a complaint online? No.

B

State Securities Administrators

Each state has its own laws and regulations for securities brokers as well as for all types of securities, including stocks, mutual funds, commodities, real estate offerings, uninsured investment products sold by banks, and others. The officials and agencies listed in this appendix enforce these laws and regulations. Many of these offices can provide you with information to help you make informed investment decisions.

State securities agencies are also responsible for preventing fraud and abuse in the sale of all but the largest securities offerings. If you have a question or complaint about an investment you have made or are about to make, call the company or bank involved. If your complaint or question is not resolved, call the appropriate state securities agency.

Alabama

Director
Securities Commission
770 Washington Avenue
Suite 570
Montgomery, AL 36130
334-242-2984
800-222-1253 (in Alabama)
www.asc.state.al.us

Alaska

Senior Examiner
Department of Commerce and Economic
　Development
P.O. Box 110807
150 3rd Street
Room 217
Juneau, AK 99801
907-465-2521
888-925-2521
www.dced.state.ak.us/bsc/bsc.htm

Arizona

Director of Securities
Arizona Corporation Commission
Securities Division
1300 West Washington
3rd Floor
Phoenix, AZ 85007
602-542-4242
www.ccsd.cc.state.az.us

Arkansas

Securities Division
Heritage West Building
201 East Markham
3rd Floor
Little Rock, AR 72201
501-324-9260
800-981-4429
www.arkansas.gov/arsec

California

Securities Regulation Division
California Corporations Commissioner
Department of Corporations
1515 K Street
Suite 200
Sacramento, CA 95814
916-327-7585
866-275-2677
www.corp.ca.gov

Colorado

Securities Commissioner
Colorado Division of Securities
1560 Broadway
Suite 900
Denver, CO 80203
303-894-2320
www.dora.state.co.us/securities

Connecticut

Banking Commissioner
Department of Banking
260 Constitution Plaza
Hartford, CT 06103
860-240-8299
800-831-7225
www.state.ct.us/dob

Delaware

Securities Commissioner
Department of Justice
Division of Securities
State Office Building
820 North French Street
5th Floor
Wilmington, DE 19801
302-577-8424
www.state.de.us/securities

District of Columbia

Commissioner
Department of Insurance and Securities
  Regulation
810 1st Street, NW
Suite 701
Washington, DC 20002
202-727-8000
http://disb.dc.gov

Florida

Chief Financial Officer
Department of Financial Services
200 East Gaines Street
Tallahassee, FL 32399
850-410-9805
800-342-2762 (in Florida)
www.dbf.state.fl.us
www.fldfs.com

Georgia

Division of Securities and Business
  Regulation
Office of the Secretary of State
802 West Tower
Two Martin Luther King, Jr. Drive, SE
Atlanta, GA 30334
404-656-3920
888-733-7427
www.sos.state.ga.us

Hawaii

Commissioner of Securities
Department of Commerce and Consumer
  Affairs
Business Registration Division
335 Merchant Street
Room 204
Honolulu, HI 96813
808-586-2744
www.hawaii.gov

Idaho
Bureau Chief
Securities Bureau
P.O. Box 83720
Boise, ID 83720-0031
208-332-8004
888-346-3378 (in Idaho)
www.state.id.us./finance/dof.htm
http://finance.idaho.gov

Illinois
Illinois Secretary of State
Securities Department
Jefferson Terrace
300 West Jefferson
Suite 300 A
Springfield, IL 62702
217-782-2256
800-628-7937 (in Illinois)
www.sos.state.il.us

Indiana
Securities Commissioner
Securities Division
Office of the Secretary of State
302 West Washington
Room E-111
Indianapolis, IN 46204
317-232-6681
800-223-8791 (in Indiana)
www.state.in.us/sos

Iowa
Enforcement Section
Iowa Securities Bureau
Enforcement Section
330 Maple Street
Des Moines, IA 50319
515-281-4441
800-351-4665
www.iid.state.ia.us/division/securities/
default.asp

Kansas
Commissioner
Office of the Kansas Securities
Commissioner
618 South Kansas Avenue
2nd Floor
Topeka, KS 66603
785-296-3307
800-232-9580 (in Kansas)
www.ink.org/public/ksecom

Kentucky
Commissioner
Department of Financial Institutions
1025 Capitol Center Drive
Suite 200
Frankfort, KY 40601
502-573-3390
800-223-2579
www.kfi.ky.gov

Louisiana

Deputy Commissioner of Securities
Office of Financial Institutions
    Securities Division
8660 United Plaza Boulevard
2nd Floor
P.O. Box 94095
Baton Rouge, LA 70804
225-925-4660
www.ofi.state.la.us

Maine

Supervisor of Enforcement
Bureau of Banking
Securities Division
121 State House Station
Augusta, ME 04333
207-624-8551
800-624-8551 (in Maine)
www.mainesecuritiesreg.org

Maryland

Securities Commissioner
Office of the Attorney General
Securities
200 Saint Paul Place
20th Floor
Baltimore, MD 21202
410-576-6360
888-743-0023
www.oag.state.md.us/securities

Massachusetts

Secretary of the Commonwealth
Securities Division
One Ashburton Place
Room 1701
Boston, MA 02108
617-727-3548
800-269-5428 (in Massachusetts)
www.state.ma.us/sec/sct

Michigan

Office of Financial and Insurance Services
P.O. Box 30220
Lansing, MI 48909
517-373-0220
877-999-6442
www.michigan.gov/cis

Minnesota

Commissioner of Commerce
Department of Commerce
85 7th Place East
Suite 500
St. Paul, MN 55101
651-296-4026
800-657-3602 (in Minnesota)
www.commerce.state.mn.us

Mississippi

Assistant Secretary of State
Mississippi Secretary of State's Office
Business Regulation and Enforcement
P.O. Box 136
Suite 500
Jackson, MS 39205
601-359-1350
800-256-3494
www.sos.state.ms.us

Missouri

Commissioner of Securities
P.O. Box 1276
Jefferson City, MO 65102
573-751-4136
800-721-7996 (in Missouri)
http://ago.missouri.gov/divisions/
    consumerprotection.htm

Montana

State Auditor & Securities Commissioner
Securities Division
Office of the State Auditor
840 Helena Avenue
Helena, MT 59601
406-444-2040
800-332-6148 (in Montana)
www.state.mt.us/sao

Nebraska

Assistant Director
Department of Banking & Finance
Bureau of Securities
The Atrium
1200 N Street
Suite 311
Lincoln, NE 68509
402-471-3445
www.ndbf.org

Nevada

Chief Compliance Enforcement
    Investigator Securities Division
Office of the Secretary of State
555 East Washington Avenue
Suite 5200
Las Vegas, NV 89101
702-486-2440
800-758-6440
www.sos.state.nv.us

Reno

Criminal Investigator III
Nevada Secretary of State
Securities Enforcement
1105 Terminal Way
Suite 211
Reno, NV 89502
775-688-1855
800-758-6440
www.sos.state.nv.us

New Hampshire

Director of Securities
Bureau of Securities Regulation
Department of State
State House
107 North Main Street
Room 204
Concord, NH 03301
603-271-1463
www.sos.nh.gov/securities

New Jersey

Bureau Chief
Department of Law and Public Safety
Division of Consumer Affairs
Bureau of Securities
153 Halsey Street
6th Floor
Newark, NJ 07102
973-504-3600
www.state.nj.us/lps/ca/home.htm

New Mexico

Regulation & Licensing Department
Securities Division
725 St. Michaels Drive
Santa Fe, NM 87505
505-827-7140
www.rld.state.nm.us

New York

Bureau Chief
New York State Department of Law
Bureau of Investor Protection and
    Securities
Office of the Attorney General
120 Broadway
23rd Floor
New York, NY 10271
212-416-8200
www.oag.state.ny.us

North Carolina

Secretary of State
Securities Division
P.O. Box 29622
Raleigh, NC 27626
919-733-3924
800-688-4507
www.sosnc.com

North Dakota

North Dakota Securities Commissioner
State Capitol
5th Floor
600 East Boulevard Avenue
Department 414
Bismarck, ND 58505
701-328-2910
800-297-5124 (in North Dakota)
www.state.nd.us/securities

Ohio

Commissioner
Division of Securities
77 South High Street
22nd Floor
Columbus, OH 43215
614-644-7381
800-788-1194
www.securities.state.oh.us

Oklahoma

Administrator
Department of Securities
First National Center
120 North Robinson
Suite 860
Oklahoma City, OK 73102
405-280-7700
Fax: 405-280-7742
www.securities.state.ok.us

Oregon

Administrator
Division of Finance & Corporate
    Securities
350 Winter Street, NE
Room 21
Salem, OR 97310
503-378-4387
503-378-4140
www.cbs.state.or.us/external/dfcs/
    index.html

Pennsylvania

Personnel Director
Pennsylvania Securities Commission
Management Services
Eastgate Office Building
2nd Floor
1010 North 7th Street
Harrisburg, PA 17102
717-783-4689
877-881-6388 (in Pennsylvania)
www.psc.state.pa.us

Rhode Island

Associate Director and Superintendent of
    Securities
Department of Business Regulation
Securities Division
233 Richmond Street
Suite 232
Providence, RI 02903
401-222-3048
www.dbr.state.ri.us

South Carolina

Deputy of Securities Commissioner
Attorney Generals Office
Securities Division
P.O. Box 11549
Columbia, SC 29211
803-734-9916
www.scsecurities.org

South Dakota

Director
Division of Securities
445 West Capitol Avenue
Pierre, SD 57501
605-773-4823
www.state.sd.us/dcr/securities

Tennessee

Assistant Commissioner
Tennessee Department of Commerce and
   Insurance—Securities
Davy Crockett Tower
Suite 680
500 James Robertson Parkway
Nashville, TN 37243
615-741-2947
800-863-9117 (in Tennessee)
www.state.tn.us/commerce

Texas

Securities Commissioner
State Securities Board
P.O. Box 13167
Austin, TX 78711
512-305-8300
www.ssb.state.tx.us

Utah

Director
Utah Department of Commerce
Division of Securities
160 East 300 South
2nd Floor
P.O. Box 146760
Salt Lake City, UT 84114
801-530-6600
800-721-7233 (in Utah)
www.commerce.state.ut.us

Vermont

Deputy Commissioner for Securities
Vermont Department of Banking,
   Insurance, Securities, & Health Care
   Administration
Securities Division
89 Main Street
Drawer 20
Montpelier, VT 05620
802-828-3420
www.bishca.state.vt.us

Virginia

Director
Division of Securities and Retail
    Franchising
State Corporation Commission
P.O. Box 1197
Richmond, VA 23218
804-371-9051
800-552-7945 (in Virginia)
www.state.va.us/scc/division/srf

Washington

Administrator
Department of Financial Institutions
Securities
P.O. Box 9033
Olympia, WA 98507
360-902-8760
www.wa.gov/dfi/securities

West Virginia

Deputy Commissioner of Securities
Securities Division
State Capitol Building 1
Room W100
Charleston, WV 25305
304-558-2257
888-368-9507
www.wvauditor.com

Wisconsin

Administrator
Division of Securities
Department of Financial Institutions
P.O. Box 1768
Madison, WI 53702
608-266-1064
800-47-CHECK (in Wisconsin)
www.wdfi.org

Wyoming

Secretary of State
Securities Division
State Capitol Building
200 West 24th Street
Cheyenne, WY 82002
307-777-7370
http://soswy.state.wy.us

C

State Department of Insurance Regulators

The sale of insurance is regulated by each state. Contacting your state regulator is the next step to follow if your complaint letter has not produced a satisfactory result. Many states have websites that have online complaint forms. This appendix contains a list of insurance regulators for each state.

There are many types of insurance: auto, home, business, life, health, casualty (accident), credit life, nursing home, boat, motorcycle, and others. Always keep a copy of your policy. Your insurance company may alter the terms of your policy by sending amendments to you tucked inside a bill or another notice. These are very important and must be saved along with the policy. The policy is a contract between you and the insurance company. The terms of your contract are contained in the policy. Read the terms of the policy carefully.

Contact your insurance agent for help. Many problems can be resolved with the help of your agent.

Alabama

Alabama Department of Insurance
Life and Health Division
P.O. Box 303351
Montgomery, AL 36130
334-241-4141
www.aldoi.org

Alaska

Alaska Division of Insurance
Consumer Services Section
550 West 7th Avenue
Suite 1560
Anchorage, AK 99501
907-269-7900
800-INSURAK (in Alaska)
www.dced.state.ak.us/insurance/
    complaintform.htm

Arizona

Department of Insurance
2910 North 44th Street
Suite 210
Phoenix, AZ 85018
602-912-8444
800-325-2548
www.id.state.az.us

Arkansas

Arkansas Insurance Department
Consumer Services Division
112 West 3rd Street
Little Rock, AR 72201
501-371-2640
800-852-5494
www.state.ar.us/insurance

California

California Department of Insurance
Consumer Services and Market Conduct
    Branch
Consumer Services Division
300 South Spring Street
South Tower
Los Angeles, CA 90013
800-927-HELP
www.insurance.ca.gov

Colorado

Department of Insurance
1560 Broadway
Suite 850
Denver, CO 80202
303-894-7499
800-930-3745
www.dora.state.co.us/insurance

Connecticut

Department of Insurance
Consumer Affairs Department
P.O. Box 816
Harford, CT 06142
860-297-3900
800-203-3447
www.state.ct.us/cid

Delaware

Department of Insurance
841 Silver Lake Boulevard
Dover, DE 19904
302-739-6775
800-282-8611 (in Delaware)
www.state.de.us/inscom

District of Columbia

Department of Insurance and Securities
   Regulation
810 1ˢᵗ Street, NE
Suite 701
Washington, DC 20002
202-727-8000
www.disb.dc.gov

Florida

Office of Insurance Registration
Department of Financial Services
200 East Gaines Street
Tallahassee, FL 32399
850-413-3100
800-342-2762
www.fldfs.com

Georgia

Two Martin Luther King, Jr. Drive
West Tower
Suite 704
Atlanta, GA 30334
404-656-2070
800-656-2298
www.gainsurance.org

Hawaii

Hawaii Insurance Division
Investigative Branch
P.O. Box 3614
Honolulu, HI 96811
808-586-2790
www.state.hi.us/dcca/ins

Idaho

Idaho Department of Insurance
Attention: Consumer Assistance
P.O. Box 83720
Boise, ID 83720
800-721-3272
www.doi.state.id.us

Illinois

Illinois Department of Insurance
320 West Washington Street
Springfield, IL 62767
866-445-5364
www.ins.state.il.us

Indiana

Indiana Department of Insurance
Consumer Services
311 West Washington Street
Suite 300
Indianapolis, IN 46204
317-232-2385
800-622-4461 (in Indiana)
www.in.gov/idoi

Iowa

Iowa Insurance Division
330 Maple Street
Des Moines, IA 50319
877-955-1212
515-281-5705 (Des Moines area)
www.iid.state.ia.us

Kansas

Kansas Insurance Department
420 SW 9th Street
Topeka, Kansas 66612
800-432-2484
www.ksinsurance.org

Kentucky

Office of Insurance
215 West Main Street
Frankfort, KY 40601
502-564-3630
800-595-6053
http://doi.ppr.ky.gov

Louisiana

Louisiana Department of Insurance
1702 North 3rd Street
Baton Rouge, LA 70802
800-259-5300
www.ldi.la.gov

Maine

Bureau of Insurance
34 State House Station
Augusta, ME 04333
800-300-5000
207-624-8475
www.MaineInsuranceReg.org

Maryland

Maryland Insurance Administration
525 St. Paul Place
Baltimore, MD 21202
410-468-2000
800-492-6116
www.mdinsurance.state.md.us

Massachusetts

Department of Insurance
Consumer Service Section
One South Street
5th Floor
Boston, MA 02110
617-521-7777
www.state.ma.us/doi

Michigan

Financial and Insurance Services
P.O. Box 30220
Lansing, MI 48909
877-999-6442
www.michigan.gov/cis

Minnesota

Minnesota Department of Commerce
85 7th Place East
Suite 500
St. Paul, MN 55101
651-297-7161
800-657-3602
www.commerce.state.mn.us

Mississippi

Mississippi Insurance Department
1001 Woolfolk State Office Building
501 North West Street
Jackson, MS 39201
800-562-2957
www.doi.state.ms.us

Mail complaints to:
Mississippi Insurance Department
Consumer Services Division
P.O. Box 79
Jackson, MS 39205

Missouri

Missouri Department of Insurance
301 West High Street
P.O. Box 690
Jefferson City, Missouri 65102
573-751-4126
800-726-7390
www.insurance.state.mo.us

Montana

840 Helena Avenue
Helena, MT 59601
800-332-6148
406-444-2040
http://sao.state.mt.us

Nebraska

Terminal Building
941 O Street
Suite 400
Lincoln, NE 68508
402-471-2201
877-564-7323
www.nol.org/home/ndoi

Nevada

Carson City Office:

788 Fairview Drive
Suite 300
Carson City, NV 89701
775-687-4270
http://doi.state.nv.us

Las Vegas Office:

2501 East Sahara Avenue
Suite 302
Las Vegas, NV 89104
702-486-4009

New Hampshire

Insurance Department
21 South Fruit Street
Suite 14
Concord NH 03301
800-852-3416
603-271-2261
www.state.nh.us/insurance

New Jersey

Division of Insurance
P.O. Box 325
Trenton, NJ 08625
609-292-5360
609-292-5316
www.njdobi.org

New Mexico

P.E.R.A. Building
1120 Paseo de Peralta
Santa Fe, NM 87504
505-827-4601
www.nmprc.state.nm.us/insurance/
    inshm.htm

New York

New York Department of Insurance
One Commerce Plaza
Albany, NY 12257
518-474-6600
800-342-3736
www.ins.state.ny.us

North Carolina

North Carolina Department of
  Insurance
1201 Mail Service Center
Raleigh, NC 27699
800-546-5664
919-733-2032
www.ncdoi.com

North Dakota

North Dakota Department of Insurance
State Capitol
600 E Boulevard
5th Floor
Bismarck, ND 58505
800-247-0560
www.state.nd.us/ndins

Ohio

Ohio Department of Insurance
Consumer Services
2100 Stella Court
Columbus, OH 43215
800-686-1526
614-644-2658
www.ohioinsurance.gov

Oklahoma

Shepherd Mall Office:
2401 NW 23rd
Suite 28
Oklahoma City, OK 73152
405-521-2828
800-522-0071
www.oid.state.ok.us

Tulsa Office:
4157 South Harvard
Suite 121
Tulsa, OK 74135
918-747-7700
800-728-2906

Oregon

Oregon Insurance Division
P.O. Box 14480
Salem, OR 97309-0405
503-947-7980
www.cbs.state.or.us/external/ins

Pennsylvania

Harrisburg:
Room 1321
Strawberry Square
Harristown State Office Building #1
Harrisburg, PA 17120
717-787-2317
www.ins.state.pa.us/ins

Philadelphia:

Room 1701
State Office Building
1400 Spring Garden Street
Philadelphia, PA 19130
215-560-2630

Pittsburgh:

Room 304
State Office Building
300 Liberty Avenue
Pittsburgh, PA 15222
412-565-5020

Rhode Island

Department of Business Regulation
Insurance Division
223 Richmond Street
Suite 233
Providence, RI 02903
401-222-2223
www.dbr.state.ri.us/insurance.html

South Carolina

South Carolina Department of Insurance
300 Arbor Lake Drive
Suite 1200
Columbia, SC 29223
803-737-6180
800-768-3467
www.doi.sc.gov

South Dakota

Department of Insurance
445 East Capitol Avenue
Pierre, SD 57501
605-773-3563
www.state.sd.us/drr2/reg/insurance

Tennessee

Department of Commerce & Insurance
500 James Robertson Parkway
4th Floor
Nashville, TN 37243
615-741-2241
www.state.tn.us/commerce/insurance/
    index.html

Texas

Texas Department of Insurance
333 Guadalupe
Austin, TX 78701
512-463-6169
800-252-3439
800-578-4677
www.tdi.state.tx.us/consumer/
    indexc.html

Utah

Utah Insurance Department
State Office Building
Room #3110
Salt Lake City, UT 84114
800-439-3805
801-538-3805
www.insurance.utah.gov

Vermont

Insurance Division
Department of Banking, Insurance,
    Securities & Health Care
    Administration
89 Main Street
Drawer 20
Montpelier, VT 05620
802-828-3302
800-964-1784
www.bishca.state.vt.us/InsurDiv/
    insur_index.htm

Virginia

Bureau of Insurance
State Corporation Commission
P.O. Box 1157
Richmond, VA 23218
804-371-9967
800-552-7945
www.state.va.us/scc

Washington

Office of Insurance
Commissioner Mike Kreidler
P.O. Box 40256
Olympia, WA 98504
360-725-7080
800-562-6900
www.insurance.wa.gov/consumers/
    complaint.asp

West Virginia

West Virginia Department of Insurance
1124 Smith Street
Charleston, WV 25301
888-879-9842
www.wvinsurance.gov

Wisconsin

Office of the Commissioner of Insurance
125 South Webster Street
Madison, WI 53702
608-266-3586 (in Madison)
800-236-8517 (statewide)
http://oci.wi.gov

Wyoming

Department of Insurance
Herschler Building
3rd Floor East
122 West 25th Street
Cheyenne, WY 82002
307-777-7401
800-438-5768 (in Wyoming)
http://insurance.state.wy.us

D

State Do Not Call Information

Each state has its own rules about the Do Not Call Registry. Many states have dropped their individual registries since the federal registry opened in June 2003. Some states have their own registries *and* their own enforcement methods. Everyone is entitled to use the federal Do Not Call Registry regardless of the state in which he or she lives. If you sign up for the federal Do Not Call Registry, you will receive full protection of this law. The federal Do Not Call law is regulated by the Federal Trade Commission (FTC). Registration is free.

Alabama
Adopted FTC program.

Alaska
Will not adopt FTC program.

State residents must register separately for FTC and state lists.

To register for Alaska program online: www.law.state.ak.us/consumer/tele_alaska.html

Arizona
Adopted FTC program.

Arkansas
Adopted FTC program and maintains own state list.

To register for Arkansas program online: www.donotcall.org

California
Adopted FTC program.

Will share names already registered on state list.

Colorado
Adopted FTC program and maintains own state list.

To register for Colorado program online: www.coloradonocall.com

Connecticut
Adopted FTC program.

Will share names already registered on state list.

Delaware
No state law. FTC registry only.

District of Columbia
No district law. FTC registry only.

Florida
Adopted FTC program and maintains own state list.

To register for Florida program online: www.800helpfla.com

Georgia
Will not adopt FTC program.

State residents must register separately for FTC and state lists.

To register for Georgia program online: www.ganocall.com

Hawaii
No state law. FTC registry only.

Idaho
Will not adopt FTC program.

State residents must register separately for FTC and state lists.

To register for Idaho program online: www.state.id.us/ag

Illinois
Adopted FTC program.

Will share names already registered on state list.

Indiana

Will not adopt FTC program.

State residents must register separately for FTC and state lists.

To register for Indiana program online: www.in.gov/attorneygeneral/consumer/telephone

Iowa

No state law. FTC registry only.

Kansas

Adopted FTC program.

Will share names already registered on state list.

Kentucky

Adopted FTC program and maintains own state list.

Will share names already registered on state list.

To register for Kentucky program online: http://nocall.ky.gov

Louisiana

Will not adopt FTC program.

State residents must register separately for FTC and state lists.

To register for Louisiana program online: www.lpsc.org/donotindex.asp

Maine

Adopted FTC program.

Will share names already registered on state list.

Maryland

No state law. FTC registry only.

Massachusetts

Adopted FTC program and maintains own state list.

Will share names already registered on state list.

To register for Massachusetts program online: https://www.madonotcall.govconnect.com

Michigan

Adopted FTC program.

Minnesota

Adopted FTC program and maintains own state list.

Will share state list with FTC.

To register for Minnesota program online: www.state.mn.us

Mississippi

Will not adopt FTC program.

State residents must register separately for FTC and state lists.

To register for Mississippi program online: www.ms.gov/psc/nocall

Missouri

Will not adopt FTC program.

State residents must register separately for FTC and state lists.

To register for Missouri program online: www.ago.mo.gov/nocalllaw/ nocalllaw.htm

Montana

Adopted FTC program.

Nebraska

Adopted FTC program.

Nevada

Adopted FTC program.

New Hampshire

No state law. FTC registry only.

New Jersey

Adopted FTC program and maintains own state list.

To register for New Jersey program online: www.nj.gov/donotcall

New Mexico

Adopted FTC program.

New York

Adopted FTC program.

Will share names already registered on state list.

North Carolina

No state law. FTC registry only.

North Dakota

Adopted FTC program.

Will share names already registered on state list.

Ohio

No state law. FTC registry only.

Oklahoma

Adopted FTC program.

Will share names already registered on state list.

To register for Oklahoma program online: www.oag.state.ok.us/oagweb.nsf/ donotcall!openpage

Oregon

Adopted FTC program.

Will share names already registered on state list.

More information about federal and Oregon do not call laws online at: www.doj.state.or.us

Pennsylvania

State program mirrors FTC program.

State residents should register for both.

To register for Pennsylvania program online: www.nocallplease.com

Rhode Island

No state law. FTC registry only.

South Carolina

No state law. FTC registry only.

South Dakota

Adopted FTC program.

Tennessee

Will not adopt FTC program.

State residents must register separately for FTC and state lists.

To register for Tennessee program online: www2.state.tn.us/tra/nocall.htm

Texas

Will not adopt FTC program.

State residents must register separately for FTC and state lists.

To register for Texas program online: www.texasnocall.com

Utah

Will not adopt FTC program.

State residents must register separately for FTC and state lists.

To register for Utah program online: consumerprotection.utah.gov/dontcall

Vermont

Adopted FTC program.

Will not share names already registered on state list.

Virginia

No state law. FTC registry only.

Washington

No state law. FTC registry only.

West Virginia

No state law. FTC registry only.

Wisconsin

Will not adopt FTC program.

State residents must register separately for FTC and state lists.

To register for Wisconsin program online: https://nocall.wisconsin.gov/web/home.asp

Wyoming

Will not adopt FTC program.

State residents must register separately for FTC and state lists.

Contact Wyoming Attorney General's office for further information.

E
Federal Agencies Consumers Should Know

Following is a list of useful federal agencies for consumers. The maze of government bureaucracy is difficult to navigate. Each office regulates a different area of commerce. Sometimes, the responsibility overlaps several agencies. The website for each office contains a mission statement or other information explaining the work each government department performs. Some agencies have local offices. When possible, consult a local office in your area.

Better Business Bureau

4200 Wilson Boulevard
Suite 800
Arlington, VA 22203-1838
www.bbb.org
File a complaint online? Yes.
Purpose: Private nonprofit organization founded in 1912 in U.S. and Puerto Rico dedicated to voluntary resolution of business/consumer problems. Maintains registry of complaints about businesses. Provides consumer education.

Comptroller of the Currency

1301 McKinney Street

Suite 3450

Houston, TX 77010

800-613-6743

www.occ.treas.gov

File Complaints Online? Yes.

Purpose: The Office of the Comptroller of the Currency (OCC) charters, regulates, and supervises all national banks. It also supervises the federal branches and agencies of foreign banks. (If your bank has the word "National" in the title, it is probably a National Bank, subject to the control of the Comptroller of the Currency, a United States agency.)

Consumer Product Safety Commission

4330 East West Highway

Bethesda, MD 20814

301-504-7923

800-638-2772

www.cpsc.gov

File a complaint online? No.

Purpose: Federal agency that protects consumers from unsafe products which may result in injury or death.

Department of Transportation

400 7th Street, SW

Washington, DC 20590

202-366-4000

www.dot.gov/citizen_services/index.html

File a complaint online? No.

Purpose: Develops and regulates transportation system in the United States.

Federal Aviation Administration (FAA)

Consumer Hotline, AOA-20

800 Independence Avenue, SW

Washington, DC 20591

866-TELL-FAA (866-835-5322)

www.faa.gov

File a complaint online? No.

Purpose: Regulates safety and efficiency of United States aerospace system for both passengers and freight, including such issues as cell phone use in flight, baggage size requirements, and baggage handling.

Federal Communications Commission (FCC)

Consumer & Governmental Affairs Bureau

Consumer Inquiries and Complaints Division

445 12th Street, SW

Washington, DC 20554

Consumer Hotline: 888-225-5322 (888-CALL-FCC)

www.fcc.gov

File Complaint Online? Yes.

Purpose: An independent United States government agency which regulates international and interstate (including possessions of the U.S.) communications by radio, television, wire, satellite, and cable. FCC regulates junk fax messages, pre-recorded telephone messages, "slamming," which is the practice of changing your telephone service without your permission, complaints about television content, and other issues important to consumers.

Federal Deposit Insurance Corporation (FDIC)

Consumer Response Center

2345 Grand Avenue

Suite 100

Kansas City, MO 64108-2638

800-378-9581

www.fdic.gov

File a complaint online? Yes.

Purpose: Independent United States agency that insures money deposited in a federally insured bank. There is a $100,000 limit for you or your family's deposit accounts at each federally insured bank. Self-directed retirement account deposits are insured for up to $250,000 limit at each federally insured bank. If a bank insured by the FDIC fails, you will be insured for the loss of the funds up to the applicable limits. Please check the FDIC website for details on your accounts.

Federal Reserve Board

Board of Governors of the Federal Reserve System

Division of Consumer and Community Affairs

20th and C Streets, NW

Stop 801

Washington, DC 20551

202-452-3693

www.federalreserve.gov/pubs/complaints

File a complaint online? No.

Purpose: Regulates state banks and their banking and lending practices. Also check your state's banking commission or department for further information.

Federal Trade Commission

CRC-240
Washington, DC 20580
877-FTC-HELP (382-4357)
www.ftc.gov/ftc/consumer.htm
File a complaint online? Yes.

Purpose: Regulates federal trade and commerce and commission rules. Includes such areas as credit, collection agencies, automobiles, advertising, financial institutions, lending practices, identity theft, telemarketing, franchises, and other common consumer problems.

Food and Drug Administration

5600 Fishers Lane
Rockville, MD 20857
888-INFO-FDA (463-6332)
www.fda.gov
File a complaint online? Yes.

Purpose: This is the oldest federal government consumer agency. The FDA protects the public health by regulating the safety and security of food, drugs for humans and animals, cosmetics, and devices which emit radiation. The agency also regulates the development and introduction of new medications. The FDA regulates hearing aids, vitamins, dietary supplements, pacemakers, contact lenses, vaccines, and blood products, among other items.

Internal Revenue Service—Taxpayer Advocate Service

877-777-4778
www.irs.gov/advocate
Call or visit the website for more information on where and how to file.

Purpose: The Taxpayer Advocate Service is an IRS program that provides an independent system to assure that tax problems, which have not been resolved through normal channels, are promptly and fairly handled.

Joint Commission on Accreditation of Healthcare Organizations (JCAHO)

One Renaissance Boulevard

Oakbrook Terrace, IL 60181

630-792-5000

800-994-6610

www.jointcommission.org

File a complaint online? Yes.

Purpose: Accredits health care institutions and organizations nationwide, including hospitals, surgical centers, home health care organizations, and ambulatory care facilities.

National Association of Insurance Commissioners (NAIC)

2301 McGee Street

Suite 800

Kansas City, MO 64108-2662

816-842-3600

www.naic.org

File Complaint Online? Yes.

Purpose: Assists state insurance commissioners in serving the public interest. Provides links to each state's insurance commissioner and consumer information.

National Association of Securities Dealers (NASD)

1735 K Street, NW

Washington, DC 20006-1500

301-590-6500

www.nasd.com

File a complaint online? Yes.

Purpose: Private association which regulates the individuals and firms in the securities business in the United States. Covers mutual funds, bonds, stocks, and other financial instruments. Conducts arbitration panels for investor complaints about securities dealers and employees.

National Credit Union Association

1775 Duke Street

Alexandria, VA 22314-3428

703-518-6300

www.ncua.gov

File a complaint online? No.

Purpose: Regulates federal credit unions and insures the accounts. Accounts are insured up to $100,000 and $250,000 for personal retirement accounts. If your credit union has the word "state" in the title, it is probably a state chartered credit union. If you are not sure if your credit union is state or federally chartered, you may call your state credit union regulator or call your credit union directly.

National Highway Transportation Safety Agency (U.S. Department of Transportation)

400 Seventh Street, SW

Washington, DC 20590

888-327-4236

www.nhtsa.dot.gov

File a complaint online? Yes.

Purpose: Save lives, prevent injuries, and reduce economic costs due to road traffic crashes through education, research, safety standards, and enforcement activity.

Office of Thrift Supervision

800-842-6929

www.ots.treas.gov

File Complaint Online? No.

Purpose: Regulates savings banks, both federal and many state-chartered institutions. This is an agency of the U.S. Department of the Treasury.

Securities and Exchange Commission

100 F Street, NE

Washington, DC 20549-0213

www.sec.gov

File a complaint online? Yes.

Purpose: To protect investors; maintain fair, orderly, and efficient markets; and to encourage the growth of the securities markets.

U.S. Department of Agriculture

1400 Independence Avenue, SW

Washington, DC 20250

800-535-4555 (toll-free)

www.usda.gov

File a complaint online? No.

Purpose: Regulates safety of meat or poultry.

United States Department of Homeland Security

Washington, DC 20528

202-282-8495

www.dhs.gov

File a complaint online? Yes

Purpose: Protection of United States. Provides disaster relief, airport security, port security, and the national transportation system security. Secures borders and supervises immigration to the United States, as well as customs rules and practices.

United States Department of Labor

Frances Perkins Building

200 Constitution Avenue, NW

Washington, DC 20210

866-444-3272

www.dol.gov

File a complaint online? No

Purpose: Regulates the workplace and workers in the U.S. labor force.

U.S. Department of Transportation Aviation Consumer Protection Division

C-75

U.S. Department of Transportation

400 7ᵗʰ Street, SW

Washington, DC 20590

800-255-1111

http://airconsumer.ost.dot.gov

File a complaint online? Yes.

Purpose: Regulates and enforces air travel issues for the general public. Security issues are handled by U.S. Department of Homeland Security.

United States Postal Inspection Service

Criminal Investigations Service Center

Attention: Mail Fraud

222 South Riverside Plaza

Suite 1250

Chicago, IL 60606-6100

www.usps.com/postalinspectors

File Complaint Online? Yes.

Purpose: Protects the United States postal system and its employees from criminal activity, including fraud and theft. Also investigates crimes in which the mail is used to promote a criminal act, such as sweepstakes scams, chain letters, identity theft, stealing mail, and filling out false forwarding information.

United States Secret Service

Office of Government Liaison & Public Affairs
245 Murray Drive
Building 410
Washington, DC 20223
202-406-5708
www.ustreas.gov/usss
File a complaint online? Yes.

Purpose: Investigates financial crimes that include, but are not limited to, access device fraud, financial institution fraud, identity theft, computer fraud; and computer-based attacks on our nation's financial, banking, and telecommunications infrastructure. Investigates credit card fraud.

F
U.S. Military Consumer Service Programs

Members of the military have resources at their disposal to assist with consumer problems. The *Servicemembers' Civil Relief Act* protects members of the military on active duty from any civil legal action taken against them. Lawsuits against them for divorce, eviction from rental property costing less than $1,200 per month, and debt collections suits cannot proceed while they are on active duty.

Family Centers, located on most military installations, provide information, life skills education, and support services to military members and their families. One of the primary functions of the Family Center is to link customers with appropriate services available in the local community or through state and federal assistance programs.

Each service refers to the Family Center by a different name. If you cannot locate a Family Center, contact your respective military branch's headquarters office listed in this appendix. (The designation "DSN" preceding some of the phone numbers refers to the military phone system, and does not apply to the civilian sector.)

Access to a directory of Family Centers by service and by state is available through the *Military Family Resource Center* (MFRC) website at **www.mfrc-dodqol.org**. If you have questions concerning other services of MFRC, visit the website or email them at **mfrc@hq.odedodea.edu**.

U.S. Air Force

Family Matters Office
HQ U.S. Air Force
Force Sustainment Division
HQ F/DPDF
1040 Air Force Pentagon
Room 5C238
Washington, DC 20330-1040
703-695-0242
225-0242 (DSN)
Fax: 703-695-7262
DSN Fax: 225-7626
www.afcrossroads.com

U.S. Army

Community and Family Support Center
4700 King Street
Alexandria, VA 22302
703-681-7395
761-5375 (DSN)
Fax: 703-681-7236
DSN Fax: 761-7236
www.armymwr.com

U.S. Coast Guard

Work/Life Program
Commandant, U.S. Coast Guard
2100 Second Street, SW
Room 6320
Washington, DC 20593
202-267-6263
Fax: 202-267-4798
www.uscg.mil/hq/g-w/g-wk/wkw

U.S. Marine Corps

Personnel Services
Programs, Personnel & Family Readiness (MRT)
3280 Russell Road
Quantico, VA 22134-5103
703-784-9546
278-9501 (DSN)
Fax: 703-784-9816
DSN Fax: 278-9816
www.usmc-mccs.org

U.S. Navy

Family Service Center
HQ, FSC Support
NPC 660 FSC Branch
5720 Integrity Drive
Millington, TN 38085-6000
901-874-4328
882-4328 (DSN)
Fax: 901-874-2785
DSN Fax: 882-2785
www.lifelines2000.org

G
Automobile Manufacturers' Customer Service Departments

Car manufacturers are very eager for your business. They are usually responsive to consumer complaints about bad experiences with dealers. If there are too many complaints, the manufacturer can cancel the dealer's contract.

If you have a problem with a car purchased from a local dealer, first try to work it out with the dealer. If the problem is not resolved, contact the manufacturer's regional or national office. Start by complaining to your *zone office*. This is the regional center for the automobile manufacturer. Many complaints are resolved at this level.

If you cannot receive satisfaction at this point, then complain to the manufacturer's headquarters. Contact the customer service department or consumer relations department. If that fails, then complain to the Chief Executive Officer of the company. If you have a complaint that may require legal attention, contact the general counsel's office of the manufacturer.

If you are still unsuccessful, consider contacting the other organizations in this section that handle consumer complaints. These programs are usually called *alternative dispute resolution programs*. Generally, there are three types: arbitration, conciliation, and mediation. All three methods of dispute resolution are different. Ask for a copy of the rules of the program before you file your case. Generally, the decisions of the arbitrators are binding and must be accepted by both the customer and the business.

However, in other forms of dispute resolution, only the business is required to accept the decision. In some programs, decisions are not binding on either party.

Before contacting one of these programs, try to resolve the complaint with the company. If you still cannot resolve your problem, contact one of the third-party resolution programs. Be sure to contact your local or state consumer agency to see if your state offers state-run dispute resolution programs. If you suspect you have a vehicle problem that might fall under your state's lemon law, call your local or state consumer protection agency to find out about your rights under the lemon law.

If you have a safety problem with your vehicle, report it to the National Highway Traffic Safety Administration Auto Safety Hotline at 888-327-4236. NHTSA also provides recall and crash test information, but does not handle complaints. The administrator's website is located at **www.nhtsa.dot.gov**.

This appendix lists automobile manufacturers that offer complaint resolution. You must ask for a list of each company's rules before agreeing to submit your claim. For further information, see the government website at **www.pueblo.gsa.gov**

Automobile Customer Service Departments

Acura
Customer Relations Department
1919 Torrance Boulevard
Torrance, CA 90501-2746
800-382-2238
www.acura.com

Alfa Romeo Distributors of North America, Inc.
7454 Brokerage
Orlando, FL 32809
407-856-5000
www.alfaromeo.com

American Honda Motor Co., Inc.

Consumer Affairs Department
1919 Torrance Boulevard
Torrance, CA 90501-2746
800-999-1009
www.honda.com

American Isuzu Motors, Inc.

Owner Relations Department
13340 183rd Street
Cerritos, CA 90702-6007
800-255-6727
www.isuzu.com

American Suzuki Motor Corp.

Customer Relations Department
P.O. Box 1100
3251 East Imperial Highway
Brea, CA 92822-1100
714-572-1490
800-934-0934 (automotive only)
www.suzuki.com

Aston Martin, Jaguar, LandRover Premier Auto Group

Customer Relations Department
U.S. National Headquarters
1 Premier Place
Irvine, CA 92618
800-452-4827
www.jaguar.com

Audi of America, Inc.

Client Relations
3499 West Hamlin Road
Rochester Hills, MI 48309
800-822-2834
www.audiusa.com

BMW of North America, Inc.

300 Chestnut Ridge Road
Woodcliff Lake, NJ 07675
800-831-1117
www.bmwusa.com

Buick Division General Motors Corp.

Customer Assistance Center
P.O. Box 33136
Detroit, MI 48232-5136
800-521-7300
www.buick.com

Cadillac Motor Car Division

Customer Assistance Center
P.O. Box 33169
Detroit, MI 48232-5169
800-458-8006
www.cadillac.com

Chevrolet Motor Division, General Motors Corp.

Customer Assistance Center
P.O. Box 33170
Detroit, MI 48232-5170
800-222-1020
www.chevrolet.com

Daihatsu America, Inc.

Consumer Affairs Department
2334 Montera Drive
Hacienda Heights, CA 91745
800-777-7070
www.daihatsu.com

Daimler Chrysler Motors Corp.

For Chrysler, Plymouth, Dodge, Jeep
P.O. Box 21-8004
Auburn Hills, MI 48321-8004
800-992-1997
www.chrysler.com

Ferrari North America Inc.

250 Sylvan Avenue
Englewood Cliffs, NJ 07632
201-816-2600
www.ferrari.com

Ford Motor Company

Customer Relationship Center
16800 Executive Plaza Drive
P.O. Box 6248
Dearborn, MI 48121
800-392-3673
www.ford.com

GMC Division General Motors Corp.

Customer Assistance Center
P.O. Box 33172
Detroit, MI 48232-5172
800-462-8782
www.gmc.com

Hyundai Motor America

Consumer Affairs
10550 Talbert Avenue
P.O. Box 20850
Fountain Valley, CA 92728-0850
800-633-5151
www.hyundai.usa.com

Kia Motors America, Inc.

Consumer Assistance Center
P.O. Box 52410
Irvine, CA 92619-2410
800-333-4KIA
www.kia.com

Lexus

Toyota Motor Sales, U.S.A., Inc.
Customer Satisfaction Department
Mail Drop L203
19001 South Western Avenue
Torrance, CA 90509-2732
800-25 LEXUS
www.lexus.com

Mazda Motor of America, Inc.

Customer Relations Manager
P.O. Box 19734
Irvine, CA 92623-9734
800-222-5500
www.mazdausa.com

Mercedes Benz of North America, Inc.

Customer Assistance Center
3 Paragon Drive
Montvale, NJ 07645
800-222 0100
www.mbusa.com

Mitsubishi Motor Sales of America, Inc.

Customer Relations
6400 Katella Avenue
Cypress, CA 90630-0064
800-MITSU-2000
www.mitsubishimotors.com

Nissan North America, Inc.

Consumer Affairs Group
P.O. Box 191
Gardena, CA 90248-0191
800-647-7261
www.nissan-usa.com

Oldsmobile Division General Motors Corp.

Customer Assistance Network
P.O. Box 33171
Detroit, MI 48232-5171
800-442-6537
www.oldsmobile.com

Peugeot Motors of America, Inc.

Consumer Relations
Overlook at Great Notch
150 Clove Road
Little Falls, NJ 07424
800-345-5545
www.peugeot.com

Pontiac Division, General Motors Corp.

Customer Assistance Center
P.O. Box 33172
Detroit, MI 48232-5172
800-762-2737
www.gm.com

Porsche Cars North America, Inc.
Owner Relations
980 Hammond Drive
Suite 1000
Atlanta, GA 30328
800-545-8039
www.porsche.com

Saab Cars USA, Inc.
Customer Assistance Center
4405-A International Boulevard
Norcross, GA 30093
800-955-9007
www.saabusa.com

Saturn Corporation, Division of General Motors Corp.
Saturn Customer Assistance Center
100 Saturn Parkway
Spring Hill, TN 37174
800-553-6000
www.saturn.com

Subaru of America, Inc.
National Customer Service Center
Subaru Plaza
P.O. Box 6000
Cherry Hill, NJ 08002
800-782-2783
www.subaru.com

Toyota Motor Sales USA, Inc.
Customer Assistance Center
Department H200
19001 South Western Avenue
Torrance, CA 90509
800-331-4331
www.toyota.com

Volkswagen of America
Customer Relations
Hills Corporate Center
3499 West Hamlin Road
Rochester Hills, MI 48309
800-822-8987
www.vw.com

Volvo Cars of North America
Customer Service
P.O. Box 914
7 Volvo Drive
Building A
Rockleigh, NJ 07647-0915
800-458-1552
www.volvocars.com

Alternative Dispute Resolution Programs

Center for Auto Safety (CAS)
1825 Connecticut Avenue, NW
Suite 330
Washington, DC 20009
202-328-7700, ext. 107
www.autosafety.org

CAS advocates on behalf of consumers in auto safety and quality, fuel efficiency, emissions, and related issues. For advice on specific problems, CAS requests that consumers write a brief statement of the problem or question, include: the year, make, model of the vehicle, and a self-addressed stamped envelope.

Council of Better Business Bureaus, Inc.
4200 Wilson Boulevard
Suite 800
Arlington, VA 22203-1838
703-276-0100
800-955-5100
www.bbb.org

Office of Defects Investigation
DOT Auto Safety Hotline
400 7th Street, SW
Washington, DC 20590
888-DASH-2-DOT
800-424-9153
www.odi.nhtsa.dot.gov/ivoq

Consumers can contact the DOT Auto Safety Hotline to report safety defects in vehicles, tires, and child safety seats. Information is available about air bags, child safety seats, seat belts, and general highway safety. Consumers who experience a safety defect in their vehicle are encouraged to report the defect to the Hotline in addition to the dealer or manufacturer.

International Association of Lemon Law Administrators
www.TheLemonLaw.org

This organization supports and promotes government agencies that administer motor vehicle warranty and related laws, through the publication of a newsletter, consumer and industry education, and other intergovernmental activities.

Motorist Assurance Program

7101 Wisconsin Avenue
Suite 1200
Bethesda, MD 20814
301-634-4954
301-634-4955
www.motorist.org

MAP accredits auto repair shops that apply and follow industry developed standards for inspecting vehicles. It also meets other requirements, handles inquiries/disputes between accredited shops and customers, and offers information to consumers about how to locate a repair shop; how to talk to a technician; and, how to gain satisfaction from auto repair shops.

National Automobile Dealers Association

8400 Westpark Drive
McLean, VA 22102
703-821-7000
800-252-6232
www.nada.org

Third-party dispute resolution program administered through the National Automobile Dealers Association. Consumer information available on request.

National Institute for Automotive Service Excellence (ASE)

101 Blue Seal Drive, SE
Suite 101
Leesburg, VA 20175
703-669-6600
www.asecert.org

ASE is an independent, national, nonprofit organization founded in 1972 to help improve the quality of automotive service and repair through the voluntary testing and certification of automotive repair professionals. ASE publishes several consumer publications about auto maintenance and repair.

RV Consumer Group

P.O. Box 520
Quilcene, WA 98376
800-405-3325 (order desk)
360-765-3846
www.rv.org

Nonprofit organization dedicated to the safety of recreational vehicles.

Index

About the Author

Janet Rubel is an Illinois attorney. She is a graduate of Washington University in St. Louis and Illinois Institute of Technology Chicago—Kent School of Law. Ms. Rubel has been an adjunct faculty member at Harper College teaching probate law for paralegals, and at John Marshall Law School teaching advanced appellate practice. She has been practicing law for more years than she cares to admit.

Ms. Rubel has won some notable cases in the Illinois Appellate Court that have attracted national attention. She convinced the Illinois Appellate Court to rule that attorneys who sexually preyed on their vulnerable clients is unethical in *Marriage of Kantar*. She took the seemingly hopeless case of a woman whose divorce attorney initiated a sexual relationship with her during her divorce. This was the first time the Illinois appellate court addressed this type of problem.

Another Illinois case of note won by the author—*Greiman v. Friedman*—is a post-divorce case limiting the college education expenses a divorced parent is required to pay. She represented a father who was ordered to pay college expenses for his two daughters. Ms. Rubel persuaded the Illinois Appellate Court to limit the father's financial obligations.

Ms. Rubel is a frequent guest on radio and television programs across the country, including *Ask Heloise* radio program, *Open House* on CNN, as well as numerous early morning news programs. She has driven through a blinding snowstorm to do the Fox morning news show in Milwaukee, alongside the Milwaukee Brewers' racing sausages. Coping with these developments was never taught in law school.

Her advice on how to complain effectively has appeared in *Parents* Magazine, *AARP* Magazine, The *Chicago Tribune*, and *Parenting* Magazine.

Visit her website at:
www.101complaints.com.